Eleanor Snyder
Susan Pries

Newton, Kansas
Winnipeg, Manitoba

Published by the General Conference Mennonite Church, Commission on Education, Newton, Kansas.
Elizabeth Raid Pankratz, editor; Mary L. Gaeddert, copy editor; John Hiebert, cover and design.

Copyright © 1996 by Faith & Life Press, Newton, KS 67114. All rights reserved. No part of this publication, unless otherwise indicated, may be reproduced, stored in a retrieval system, or transmitted in any form or by any means, electronic, mechanical, photocopying, recording, or otherwise, without the prior permission of the copyright owner.

Printed in the U.S.A.

Library of Congress Number 95-61974

International Standard Book Number 0-87303-173-3

The publishers gratefully acknowledge the cooperation of individuals, publishers, and trusts who have granted permission to include copyrighted material in this book. We have carefully endeavored to ascertain the copyright status of each piece. If any songs or other material have been included without proper permission or credit, we will upon notification gladly make necessary corrections in future editions.

Table of Contents

Look It Over

Meet the writers

Eleanor Snyder serves as Director of Children's Education for the General Conference Mennonite Church, Newton, Kansas. Eleanor has been involved in Christian education in some form or another as long as she can remember—as a Sunday school teacher, club leader, youth sponsor, committee member, and conference staff person. When *Loving God* was written, she was the minister of Christian education for the Mennonite Conference of Eastern Canada.

Bloomingdale Mennonite Church in Ontario, Canada, is Eleanor's home congregation. She lives in Breslau, Ontario, and is married to Stuart Snyder. They have two young adult children, Jeff and Sheila.

In her spare time, Eleanor likes to read and cook. For fun reading, she enjoys mysteries. Books on theology, spirituality, and Christian education also capture her interest. In the food department, she especially likes to do yeast baking and preparing fancy desserts to serve when she has time for entertaining.

Susan Pries attends First Mennonite Church in Kitchener, Ontario. She has been actively involved in Christian education as a Sunday school teacher, club leader, vacation Bible school leader and coordinator, and workshop leader. Susan also uses her musical talents to serve the church. She has been involved in community service projects and activities.

Susan is married to John Pries, and the couple have three school-aged children—Rachel, Jacob, and Joshua. Serving as a volunteer and being a stay-at-home mom suit her well. She enjoys family holiday time and baking.

From the editor

Loving God is the fifth piece in the complete, freestanding curricula of the Living Stones Collection. *Loving God* was developed for several reasons. Congregations liked the format of the broadly graded groupings and unique themes that were presented in previous vacation Bible school curricula, e.g., *I Am Somebody God Loves* and *Simon Peter*.

The Loving God theme emerged out of a desire to teach children how to love God through prayer and action. The stories from Samuel aptly illustrated this two-fold expression of love for God.

In the Pray and Learn time, children learn to listen and talk to God in a number of ways. It is my hope that their communication with God will be enriched through the prayer and Bible memory activities that are offered.

Through the active games and simulation activities during Talk and Move, the children learn, in fun-loving ways, how to relate the stories from the Bible to their own situations. Talking about the experience is a very important way to apply biblical truths to everyday life.

Each session the children will make a visible reminder of God's love during Make and Take. By the end of the Loving God programme, they will have a door hanging to show how they learned about and experienced God's love during the sessions.

Worship engages the mind and the heart through the songs and Bible story dramas. Children see the biblical characters come alive and identify with the story in new ways as they consider what it means for them personally.

Elizabeth Raid Pankratz, editor

The writers encourage

Writing this curriculum was truly a collaborative effort. The creative energy of many people combined to make *Loving God* a strong, comprehensive curriculum. The Bible story dramas were written by Kathleen Cleland Moyer who retains ownership of these dramas. Elizabeth R. Eby wrote the Early Childhood Puppet Plays. A special thank-you goes to Gloria Shantz, Lois Weber, Jennifer Mains, Marie Gingerich, Mary Stewart, and Phyllis Bishop who also helped develop this curriculum.

It is our desire that you will take these ideas and add your creative energy to plan and carry out your children's programme. This curriculum is a tool to help you share the good news of God's love and develop relationships with children that will invite them to choose to love God in return for God's love of them. May you use your gifts to meet your particular needs.

It is our prayer and hope that this curriculum will help children and adults learn to know and love God as a personal friend and guide. We hope that each person involved in *Loving God* may experience God's love through prayer and action, through reflection and discussion, through music, stories, and games. Having experienced God's love, may you express the love of God in your everyday relationships with family, friends, neighbours, and strangers.

May you who lead this curriculum find that your love for God and others is enriched and expanded as you prepare to share God's love with peers and children. May you experience anew God's power and presence in your prayer and active life. May the love of God and the inspiration of God's Holy Spirit be with you as you learn together with children about our wonderful, loving God.

". . . The Lord is our God, the Lord alone. You shall love the Lord your God with all your heart, and with all your soul, and with all your might. Keep these words that I am commanding you today in your heart. Recite them to your children and talk about them when you are at home and when you are away, when you lie down and when you rise. Bind them as a sign on your hand, fix them as an emblem on your forehead, and write them on the doorposts of your house and on your gates" (Deuteronomy 6:4-9, NRSV).

Blessings and love be with you as you experience *Loving God* in new and exciting ways.

Eleanor Snyder and Susan Pries, writers

Theme

Loving God is based on five stories taken from the Old Testament books of 1 and 2 Samuel—the stories of Hannah, Samuel, Jonathan, Abigail, and David.

The title "Loving God" both describes who God is and identifies our response in life as we love God. Our God is a loving God who cares deeply for each one of us. God's love for us is limitless and unconditional. We are invited to respond to God's love with our whole being. Our love for God is expressed in our choice to follow God's way–in our prayer life, our attitude and behaviour toward others, and in the way we live every day.

Session titles and themes:

Session	Title	Theme
Session 1	Hannah	Loving God by Praying
Session 2	Samuel	Loving God by Listening
Session 3	Jonathan	Loving God by Loving Others
Session 4	Abigail	Loving God by Making Peace
Session 5	David	Loving God by Showing Kindness

Memory texts

Luke 10:27 and Micah 6:8 are the memory texts. There are additional session theme texts that are introduced and learned during Pray and Learn. The text is printed in the Pray and Learn Resource section.

Objectives

1. To provide Bible-based materials that integrate learning through worship, reflection, interaction with other people, and hands-on experiences in a variety of Christian education settings.
2. To familiarize children with the biblical characters of Hannah, Samuel, Jonathan, Abigail, and David. To help children recognize that God's love for each of these people was the same. Each person responded to God's love in a different way.
3. To encourage children to choose to love God with all their heart, soul, and strength, and to love their neighbour as themselves.
4. To help children understand that God loves them unconditionally and wants them to express their love through worship and through healthy relationships.
5. To provide a method of teaching and learning that encourages group interaction and experiential learning activities.
6. To integrate all activities under a common theme. The arts and crafts, games, songs, and story responses are all based on the daily topic. Learning in a variety of ways reinforces the theme.

Methods

Children from kindergarten age through grade 5 form small learning groups that include all these ages. The early childhood children (4- and 5-year-olds) form a separate group for their time together. The junior youth (grades 6, 7, 8) spend part of the day in separate groups for learning activities and special projects. The session texts and themes are the same for every age-group.

Included for each session are appropriate biblical texts that provide background reading for the leaders, a specific theme, a story and faith focus, song titles, Bible story dramas, and lesson plans for each of three rotating activity sessions: Talk and Move, Pray and Learn, Make and Take. For a detailed outline, see the Master Schedule, page 21.

Adapt it

Midweek program

Use *Loving God* for a five-week programme during the early evening in your community. Begin with Worship, then move into the response activities (Talk and Move, Pray and Learn, and Make and Take), either in age/grade groupings or in broadly graded groupings that rotate to several centres.

Each session stands on its own within the broader context of *Loving God.* By offering this programme once a week, children have the opportunity to reflect during the week on how each session's theme fits into the larger theme.

Summer Sunday school

Loving God will work well for a summer session. There is enough material in each session for you to spend two or three weeks on each session. Children do not mind hearing good stories over and over. Repeat the drama at the beginning of each session—children will learn more the second time. In the response time (Talk and Move, Pray and Learn, and Make and Take), you have several choices. All the children together may do the same activity from one of the resource sections. Or set up activity centres for each theme—children choose a different one each Sunday. Leaders stay with one centre, repeating the lesson each week to a different group of children.

For extra sessions, do a service project with the children, plan a celebration with the parents and congregation, or have a Loving God party!

All-church worship and education service

Choose one of the sessions for an intergenerational celebration. Begin with the Bible drama and music. To expand options: add a music centre in which a group learns several theme songs; offer a memory centre to learn memory texts in creative ways; do a service project together; expand the junior youth resources to include older youth in discussion and activity.

Weekend programme

Offer five sessions over the weekend for children or for the whole congregation, possibly one on Friday evening, two or three on Saturday, and one or two on Sunday. If this is a camping or retreat weekend where people eat and sleep at the same place, there can be flexibility in the times and lengths of sessions.

Allow for lots of group building and social activities. For planning such a weekend, have different groups be responsible for planning and conducting the sessions. Involve the children and/or families in leadership when possible.

Camping program

For a five-day camp, use the Worship Resource (pp. 33-60) at the beginning of the day to introduce the theme. In discovery or Bible time, use ideas from the Talk and Move Resource section to apply the biblical theme to the children's daily living. During craft time, do the Make and Take project of the day. At bedtime or vespers, use the prayer ideas from the Pray and Learn Resource section.

Family vacation time

Family members can practice and present the Bible dramas to each other. Read the texts from the Bible to compare with the written drama and dig deeper into the texts. Tell the story from the first-person perspective of the biblical character. Choose activities from the three age-group sections (kindergarten-grade 5, early childhood, and junior youth) that fit your family needs.

If your family prefers craft activities, pick ideas from the Make and Take Resource section. If you like playing games together, find fun things to do in the Talk and Move Resource section. For prayer time and family devotions, find activities and suggestions in the Pray and Learn Resource section.

Resource for grandparents

This curriculum is a very flexible resource. Grandparents can use it with grandchildren who spend holiday or vacation time with them. Children learn to know God and their grandparents better as they learn together about loving God.

Church-run child care programme

Use the early childhood materials for this program. Young children learn stories about God's love, and participate in a variety of activities that reinforce the story and theme.

Get It Organized

Leaders and responsibilities

If you wish to follow the basic plan for *Loving God*, you will need the following leaders:

1. *Loving God* coordinator
2. Worship coordinator
3. Talk and Move leader
4. Pray and Learn leader
5. Snack coordinator
6. Make and Take leader
7. Group leaders
8. Early Childhood leader
9. Junior Youth leader

If you have fewer leaders or wish to follow a more traditional plan, see Leader options, page 22.

Loving God coordinator

- Organize and plan the Loving God programme. Use Look It Over, pages 5-10, and Get It Organized, pages 11-31, to help you. Meet with your committee and the other leaders. Together decide how to adapt *Loving God* to fit your needs.
- Be sure all the leaders have the curriculum they need and understand their responsibilities. Check on general supply needs and help the leaders with specific requests for materials or audiovisual aids.
- Copy pages 26-29 for the Group leaders and go over these materials with them. Encourage as many people as possible to use their talents to make *Loving God* a meaningful and memorable experience.
- Register the children as they arrive on the first day. Assign them to their small group. Lists of pre-registered children can be prepared beforehand to speed up registration. You may hand out the prepared name tags or have the

children put their names on the tags themselves. If you have a large group to register, set up tables according to the ages of the children. As the children arrive, send them to the appropriate table for a name tag and group assignment. If the groups are broadly-graded (K-5), it is best to have each child with one other person she or he knows.
- Make copies of the Curriculum Evaluation Form, page 205, for all the leaders and plan how you will process the evaluation. Mail the compiled evaluation to the address on the form.

Worship coordinator

- Plan the Worship for each of your five sessions. Use the Worship Resource, pages 33-60, for complete plans and a detailed description of your responsibilities.
- Present the biblical story to the children in an engaging and meaningful way. Use the dramas as one way to relate God's story of love for humanity. Look for other creative ways to present the Bible stories that fit your group and setting.
- Learn and teach music to the children or appoint someone who is gifted in music to lead that part of the Worship.

Talk and Move leader

Detailed session plans are included in the Talk and Move Resource section, pages 61-82.

- Have good communication skills. The leader should enjoy being outdoors and playing active games. Your energy and enthusiasm help to involve the children actively.
- Encourage Group leaders to continue the discussion when their groups meet at the end of the day.
- Review the Bible story and reinforce it through active learning and simulation games.
- Begin with large muscle exercises, running games, or another activity to get the children moving.
- Discuss the children's feelings and how the activity related to the Bible story and the session's theme.

Pray and Learn leader

Detailed session plans are included in the Pray and Learn Resource section, pages 83-110.

- Have a strong personal relationship with God.
- Talk freely about that relationship and lead in prayer.
- Be inviting as you relate to the children.
- Encourage the children to participate in an activity that may or may not be familiar to them.
- Include learning the memory verses, quiet reflection and prayer, and a snack.
- Encourage the children to develop a personal relationship with God.
- Serve snacks from the suggestions on page 14.
- Engage the help of the Group leaders and encourage their continued discussion of the material you presented.

Snack coordinator

- Choose snacks that are nutritious, easy to prepare, and that the children will enjoy. Purchase and prepare the snack in consultation with the leader of Pray and Learn. Be responsible to prepare snacks and deliver them to each group at the appropriate times.

Snack suggestions:

Session 1: pretzels (not sticks)
A recipe for "Soft Pretzels" is included on page 187.

Session 2: crunchy foods—celery and carrot sticks, crackers with peanut butter, popcorn, etc.

Session 3: heart-shaped cookies
Ideas for making "Friendship Cookies" are given in the Make and Take Resource, Optional Activities, page 115.

Session 4: mini rice cakes or large crackers

Session 5: a combination of food items such as vegetables with dip, dried fruit, raisins and chocolate chips, and/or ice cream bars

- Homemade bars are easy and inexpensive to make. Purchase chocolate wafers at a bulk food store and ice cream by the 2-litre carton. Cut each carton of ice cream into bar shapes, 16 or 24 depending on the thickness of ice cream you prefer. Press two wafers on either side of the ice cream and freeze. These ice cream bars taste better if allowed to "ripen" overnight.
- Other snack choices are: nutritious cookies, apple slices with peanut butter, fresh fruit pieces, celery sticks with a cheese spread, pretzels, nuts (some children are allergic to nuts), GORM (good old raisins and M&Ms).

Make and Take leader

Detailed session plans are included in the Make and Take Resource section, pages 111-128.

- Provide hands-on art and craft activities that reinforce the theme.
- Have an interest in crafts and be able to encourage children to be creative.
- Value the individual creativity of each child.
- Engage the help of the Group leaders.

Early Childhood leaders (see pp. 130-133)

Junior Youth leaders (see pp. 178-180)

Permission is granted to those who purchase this resource to photocopy pages 14-16 for Group leaders' use only.

Group leaders (kindergarten to grade 5)

You should receive a complete list of your responsibilities (pages 14-21 of this curriculum) from the *Loving God* coordinator.

- Care about children and about God.
- Enjoy children and be a friend to them.
- Relate easily to children from a variety of homes and backgrounds.
- Accept each child as a person loved by God.

Introduction

As a Group leader, you are a very important person in this programme. You could compare yourself to a counselor at camp, one who spends quality time with children. As the adult who will spend the most time with the children in your group, you have the privilege to become a special friend and role model to the children. You will most clearly demonstrate to the children what it means to love God as a grown-up.

Although you are not involved in the major part of planning, you are responsible for community building among group members, for making each child feel accepted and welcome, and for seeing that the children cooperate and participate in the variety of activities each day.

Responsibilities

You are responsible for knowing what is happening in all areas of the programme that affect your group of children. Ask the *Loving God* coordinator for a copy of the introductory materials, including the Master Schedule. Read through this information carefully so that you know what to do and expect each day.

Early preparation and ongoing responsibilities:

1. Prepare name tags for your group members. Have markers available for them to put their names on the name tags.
2. Have registration forms ready for distribution at the end of the first day. Ask the *Loving God* coordinator for these forms.
3. Provide a container for the offering. Be familiar with the offering project and encourage the children to share the information with their parents.
4. Prepare the attendance record (page 28) and attendance charts if used. If you want a visual record for attendance, hand out heart stickers, etc., for children to stick on a bristol or poster board bookmark base, a larger heart, etc. Be creative!
5. Prepare a place to store the name tags at the end of each session. If you are using hearts, you may wish to make a larger heart of the same colour. Place the heart on the bulletin board. Arrange sturdy straight pins in the heart for the children to place their name tags at the end of the day.
6. Make your gathering place a welcoming place for your group. Whether you meet in a classroom, tent, or on a blanket out-of-doors, do whatever you can to help the children feel comfortable and at home.
7. Arrive early each day to greet and welcome the children by name. Early birds can look at books, play a game, help with name tags and attendance, etc. As children arrive, have them place their offering in the container.
8. Learn the closing blessing, "Go in Peace," with the motions, page 30. Natalie Sleeth has written a song "Go Now in Peace" that would work well for a closing blessing. This song is found in *Becoming God's Peacemakers*, Living Stones Collection (Newton, Kans.: Faith & Life Press, pp. 145-147) and *Hymnal: A Worship Book* (Elgin, Ill.: Brethren Press; Newton, Kans.: Faith & Life Press; Scottdale, Penn.: Mennonite Publishing House, p. 429).

Group-building ideas

1. Develop a group cheer. Use your group name and make a rhyming poem or a short catchy song that describes who you are.
2. If your groups are identified with a colour, have them wear a T-shirt of that colour every day. Be sensitive to children who may not have coloured T-shirts. Perhaps they can wear just one item of that colour, such as a barrette, sock, scarf, jewelry.

3. Learn about each other's favourite things. Give each person the opportunity to tell the group what is her or his favourite snack food, dessert, television show, colour, vacation spot, book, Bible story.

4. Have a daily sharing time.

- Session 1: Learn everyone's name and tell about yourself.
- Session 2: Talk about listening. Give each person thirty seconds to tell about their favourite sounds. Remind the children to listen carefully to each other.
- Session 3: Talk about friendships. Who is the child's best friend? What makes a best friend? How does one make new friends? What would one risk for a friend?
- Session 4: Invite each person to tell about a recent conflict situation and how it was resolved.
- Session 5: Talk about the meaning of "loving-kindness." Have the children tell about a time someone did something kind for them. How did it feel?

Gather and Greet (Session 1)

1. When everyone has arrived and been greeted, take the time to learn about each other. Form a circle. Go around the circle and have everyone say her or his complete name and what she or he prefers to be called. After each name is given, everyone repeats the preferred name together. Flip the name tags over so they cannot be seen. Continue around the circle a second time, having everyone give the name of the person on her or his right. Again, have all repeat the name together. Do this again to the left of the person. Next, go around the circle with the entire group shouting each person's name.

To review the names during the next sessions, use other techniques: toss a ball and have the receiver repeat the name of the person who tossed it, and the name of the person to whom the ball is being tossed; invite people to go around the circle, naming all the children; match the first letter of the first name with an activity that is enjoyed ("My name is John and I like jumping").

2. Explain your daily ritual to the children—how you wish to begin each session in your group. Explain about name tags, attendance, offering, and other activities you will do during Gather and Greet.

3. Before you go to Worship, invite the children to pray with you. Offer a simple prayer, inviting them to be open to God's presence during this session and throughout the entire programme.

4. Go together as a group to Worship.

Worship (daily)

1. Sit with your group and participate in the songs and activities. Remember that you are modeling acceptable behaviour for the children. When you become actively involved, the children will also participate. It is your responsibility to manage undesirable behaviour. Sit beside a fidgety, noisy child. If the child becomes distracting, do not hesitate to remove that child from the worship area until she or he is ready to sit quietly.

2. Listen carefully for instructions regarding the rotation to activities, etc., before dismissal, and accompany your group to the next activity.

Talk and Move (daily)

1. Accompany your group to the Talk and Move meeting place. Be a willing participant. You are the Talk and Move leader's assistant. Be prepared to lead as you are directed. Ask the leader beforehand how she or he expects you to help.

2. Talk with your group about how love for God was expressed in the story

and can be expressed in the lives of the children. Be willing to tell the group about your personal relationship with God and how you have experienced God's love. Listen to what the children say. Let them know you care about them and their relationship with God. Do not force your adult views on them. Let the Holy Spirit guide the discussion.

3. Keep an eye on the clock. Help the leader clean up and prepare for the next group. When instructed, go with your group to the next activity.

Make and Take (daily)

1. Accompany your group to the Make and Take area and offer to assist the leader in any way. Be prepared to do as instructed and help the children who require assistance. Help with the cleanup and preparation for the next group.

2. Lead your group to the next activity.

Pray and Learn (daily)

1. Learn the memory texts along with the children. Be prepared to review the texts with games, etc., during your small-group sessions at the beginning and end of the day.

2. During this time, children will be given the opportunity to reflect on their personal relationship with God and to pray. Encourage them to be respectful of others, to sit silently when requested, and to use this time to talk with God as they would with a close friend.

3. The snack time is written into this session. Sometimes snack is part of the prayer time. Check with the leader about snack details, and be prepared to serve the snack to your group. Offer your assistance and be involved actively in all of the activities.

Closing (daily)

Closing time will take place either in the large assembly group or within the small groups.

1. Review the day. Sit in a circle. Ask the children to tell what they liked best, what they are wondering about, and what the Bible story was about. Invite them to think of one thing they will tell their parents about God.

2. Pray together and review the memory text.

3. Say the closing blessing, "Go in Peace," and do the motions (see page 30).

4. Make announcements or send home reminders as needed.

5. Collect the name tags. Thank the children for coming and encourage them to come back and bring a friend.

Personal preparation

Prepare yourself for this important ministry.

- Spend time in prayer for the program, the leaders, and yourself as Group leader.
- Spend time in personal Bible study. Read the biblical texts for each day's story and reflect on what they mean for you.
- Ask the Holy Spirit to give you new insights on these stories and their effect on the children.
- Consider the faith focus for each day. How do you respond to the text? How can you help the children in your care to respond to God's love for them?

Resources

Ask the *Loving God* coordinator for the following resources:

- Master Schedule, page 21
- Registration Form, page 26
- Attendance Form, page 28
- Closing Blessing, page 30
- Bible Memory Passages, page 105
- Session Titles and Themes, pages 19-20
- Books and Audiovisuals, pages 30-31

Know the children

If you teach a broadly graded group (kindergarten to grade 5)

- Respect each child as an individual with special needs and gifts.
- Remember the broader age span and use appropriate language in your discussions and teaching.
- Encourage children to respond at their individual level of understanding.
- Encourage the active participation of each person.
- Promote group building and learning across the ages by pairing older and younger children for discussion and activity and by forming small groups that include people of each age-group for games, skits, crafts, etc.

If you teach early childhood (ages four and five)

- Demonstrate a love for young children.
- Have patience.
- Be well organized and plan ahead so that the children are cared for all the time.

Early childhood sessions are built around the same themes as those for older children. However, early childhood should hold their sessions independently. Directions for organizing the early childhood programme are found on pages 130-135 in the Early Childhood section.

If you teach primary children (kindergarten through grade 2)

Primary children think of God as a friend to whom they can talk. They have not yet developed abstract reasoning. They are usually trusting of adults. Use their spiritual understanding and provide caring and loving models that they can trust and follow. Remember that they have limited reading ability and learn best by doing and seeing.

If you teach middler children (grades 3 through 5)

Children in the middle grades are beginning to develop abstract thinking. They have a strong sense of fairness, of right and wrong. Be sure that you present the biblical concepts of God's forgiveness, of God's love and care for everyone. Model God's forgiveness and have concern for others. Include all the children in activities that meet their needs. Value their questions, and invite them to a loving relationship with Jesus who taught us how to live God's way.

If you teach junior youth (grades 6 through 8)

- Enjoy being with adolescents.
- Serve as an active listener, a discussion facilitator, a person who cares about the natural and spiritual development of the young adolescents.
- Be an advocate for the junior youth, intent on helping them to grow into a loving relationship with Jesus.
- Model a positive relationship with Jesus and be willing to talk about it with young people.
- Invite youth to ask their faith questions and do not insist on giving them the answers.
- Be willing to adapt the curriculum to the needs of the children in your care.

Session titles and themes

Session 1

Hannah

Theme: Loving God by Praying
Bible Text: 1 Samuel 1:1—2:1-11
Story Focus: Hannah's love for God was demonstrated in her prayer life. She trusted that God would answer her prayer. She fulfilled her promise to God when she took Samuel to the temple to live with Eli.
Faith Focus: We show that we love God when we talk to God. We trust that God will hear and answer us when we pray.

Session 2

Samuel

Theme: Loving God by Listening
Bible Text: 1 Samuel 2:18-21, 26; 3:1-21
Story Focus: When Samuel realized that God was calling to him, he responded by listening to God's voice.
Faith Focus: We show that we love God when we listen for God's voice and respond.

Session 3

Jonathan

Theme: Loving God by Loving Others
Bible Text: 1 Samuel 20:1-42
Bible Background: 1 Samuel 18 and 19
Story Focus: Jonathan risked his life for his best friend, David, though it meant danger for him.
Faith Focus: We show that we love God when we are a true friend.

Session 4

Abigail

Theme: Loving God by Making Peace
Bible Text: 1 Samuel 25:1-38
Story Focus: Abigail demonstrated creative thinking skills in order to keep peace between two enemies, Nabal and David.
Faith Focus: We show that we love God when we solve our problems in peaceful ways.

Session 5

David

Theme: Loving God by Showing Kindness
Bible Text: 2 Samuel 4:4; 9:1-13
Story Focus: David showed kindness when he brought Mephibosheth into his home.
Faith Focus: We show that we love God when we are kind, just, and generous.

Schedule

(kindergarten-grade 5)

This programme is designed for five sessions, each lasting two and three-quarter hours. The setting is adaptable for outdoors, indoors, or a combination of both. If your programme does not allow for this length of time, there are several options to consider: shorten Gather and Greet and Closing, shorten the time for Worship, or offer only two rotation activities. For a detailed outline, refer to the Master Schedule on page 21.

Each session follows the same outline:

- **Gather** (15 minutes)
- **Worship** (30 minutes)
- **Activity** (105 minutes)
  - Thirty-minute periods each of three activity centres, with five minutes between sessions for moving
  - **Talk and Move**
  - **Pray and Learn**
  - **Make and Take**
- **Closing** (15 minutes)

Master Schedule

15 Minutes **Gather and Greet** (Meet in small groups for attendance, offering, group building)					
30 Minutes **Worship** (Total group assembly)					
	Session 1	Session 2	Session 3	Session 4	Session 5
Themes and Bible Texts	*Hannah: Loving God by Praying* 1 Samuel 1:1—2:1-11	*Samuel: Loving God by Listening* 1 Samuel 2:18-21, 26; 3:1-21	*Jonathan: Loving God by Loving Others* 1 Samuel 20:1-42	*Abigail: Loving God by Making Peace* 1 Samuel 25:1-38	*David: Loving God by Showing Kindness* 2 Samuel 4:4; 9:1-13
Three-way Rotation (kindergarten-grade 5)					
35 Minutes **Talk and Move**	• Obstacles to Prayer Course • Hopscotch • Obstacle Toss • Discussion	• Sammy Says • Temple Pray and Learn Game • Discussion	• Three-Legged Race • Jonathan Walk • Friendship Stand	• Shake Your Bod • Abigail's Dilemma • Peace-makers' Cheer	• Frozen Tag • Feast of David Game • Soccer • Discussion
35 Minutes **Pray and Learn**	• Memory Texts • Litany of Praise • Pretzel Story • Prayer Time	• Memory Texts • Listening Activity • Prayer Time	• Memory Texts • Discussion • Letters to God Booklet	• Memory Texts • Circle Game • Peace Promise Mural	• Memory Texts • Hands Wreath • Prayer Bracelet
35 Minutes **Make and Take**	• Ongoing Door Hanging: Panel 1—Loving God title	• Panel 2—symbols of listening	• Panel 3—woven heart	• Panel 4—peace dove mosaic	• Panel 5—coupon gift box
15 Minutes **Closing** (Meet as a larger assembly or in small groups for reviewing memory work, singing, and the closing blessing.)					

Gather and Greet (15 minutes)

Each broadly graded group (one adult and up to ten children) meets individually for attendance, offering, morning prayer, and group-building activities. The group meets in the same place at the beginning in a classroom, on a blanket outside, or in an auditorium. The leader and children interact informally. The leader welcomes the children to the day's activities and does simple activities that will help the group begin to feel like a community. Each group will be given a name that identifies itself (see page 25). After everyone has gathered and the opening rituals are completed, the group goes together to the assembly area for Worship.

Worship (30 minutes)

Children from kindergarten to grade 8 meet in an assembly area to sing songs and listen to and watch the daily drama. Begin the worship with favourite and familiar "sing-along" songs. A general listing of music resources can be found on page 54.

Story is a powerful method of sharing truth with children of all ages. Five stories in the form of dramas tell about biblical characters who demonstrated their love for God in a variety of ways. The dramas are written for two to five characters. For more details about the dramas, check pages 34-53. If possible, choose a drama team to prepare and present all five dramas.

Three-way Rotation Plan (105 minutes)

After Worship, each group goes to one of the three activity centres for a thirty-minute session. Five minutes are allowed for travel time between the centres. Each group will rotate to each centre every session. Vary the rotation so that the groups will start at a different centre some days. If groups need to be combined for the rotation, be sure to put different groups together each day. Set up a chart similar to the one below to show the rotation each day.

Session 1	*Talk and Move*	*Pray and Learn*	*Make and Take*
Activity 1 (30 min.)	Groups A,B,C	Groups D,E,F	Groups G,H,I
Activity 2 (30 min.)	Groups D,E,F	Groups G,H,I	Groups A,B,C
Activity 3 (30 min.)	Groups G,H,I	Groups A,B,C	Groups D,E,F

Closing (15 minutes)

This is a time to review the session theme, sing the theme song, review the memory work, and make any announcements. If your total group is very large, you may prefer to have the small groups go to their home base to review the day's activities and memory text, or just to chat together. In either case, close with the blessing "Go in Peace," included in the Resource section. If you use the song (see page 54) teach it to the whole group on the first day.

To reduce the overall time, you may eliminate the Closing. Children return to their home base at the end of the rotation time, sing the blessing together, then disperse for home.

Leader options

If you teach the complete session for one age or grade

- Early Childhood: Use the Early Childhood section, pages 129-176.
- Kindergarten-grade 2: Use the daily session plans for Gather and Greet, Worship, Talk and Move, Pray and Learn, Make and Take, and Closing.

- Grades 3-5: Use the daily session plans for Gather and Greet, Worship, Then and Now, Games and Snack, Make and Take, and Closing.
- Grades 6-8: Use the Junior Youth section, pages 177-204.
  Follow the three-way rotation plan with your individual grade.

If you lead Worship, Talk and Move, Pray and Learn, or Make and Take

- Follow the daily session plans in your corresponding resource section. See the Table of Contents, pages 3 and 4.

To set up a Three-way Rotation Plan for kindergarten through grade 5

This plan works best with three groups of equal numbers, up to thirty in each group.

- See the Three-way Rotation Plan, page 22. Change the rotation pattern each day.

Age/grade groupings

Early Childhood

Children of ages four and five participate in the early childhood programme. They are assigned to a small group with an adult leader. They do not need to be separated by ages. A separate curriculum has been prepared using the same session themes (see pages 129-176). It is recommended that the early childhood programme be separate in all aspects.

Kindergarten through grade 5

Children who have completed kindergarten through grade 5 make up the second group of children. Assign them to small groups made up of one adult and no more than ten children. Groups can be arranged in broadly graded groupings by having an equal number of children from each grade in each small group, or divide into younger (K, 1, 2) and older age-groups (3, 4, 5). If the groups are larger than ten members, it becomes more difficult to develop close relationships.

Because a three-way rotation is offered, this programme operates best if the groupings are in multiples of three. For each of the rotation activities, up to three groups can be combined. For example, if there are ninety children in the K-5 age-group, three groups of ten participants would be in Talk and Move, three groups in Make and Take, and three in Pray and Learn. Each day, different groups can be placed together in the rotation schedule. If there are more than ninety children, it is recommended that two rotation schedules be developed to run concurrently.

Junior youth

Children who have completed grades 6, 7, and 8 form a separate group for part of the programme. This group remains together regardless of size. However, have an adult group leader for each group of ten participants. A junior youth supplement is included in this curriculum (see pages 177-204). Junior youth participate as a separate group for Gather and Bless and during the rotation activities when they have their own Bible study and response activities. Junior youth participate with kindergarten through grade 5 for Worship and may or may not be part of Closing.

Additional helps

Logo

The logo (page 29) simply reflects the theme of loving God. The linking hearts symbolize our desire to be connected to God by love. Use the logo patterns provided for posters and other announcements of the *Loving God* event for name tags, for T-shirt decorations, and in other ways to link a visual image to your programme.

Extra activities

Plan for those unexpected times when the programme plans must be changed. A listing of books and audiovisuals is included in Resources, pages 30-31. If there is extra time in the Make and Take and Pray and Learn activities, have some of these books and resources available for use by the children.

Library resources

Ask your church librarians to preview and purchase some of the books listed. Use them for your programme and offer them to the children throughout the year. A list of recommended books for kindergarten through junior youth appears on pages 30-31 and for early childhood, pages 167-168.

Make and Take choices

If the door-hanging does not appeal to you, choose some other crafts. Be sure that they reinforce the theme of loving God. The craft should be an ongoing reminder to the children of God's love and the stories of God's people who experienced that love.

Group names

Group names may be used to identify the small groups. Children are assigned to a group with a Group leader and an identifying name. Group names can be as simple as colours. Or identify the groups with the Bible characters, such as House or Clan of Hannah, Samuel, Jonathan, Abigail, and David. If there are more than five groups, use other Bible characters. Include both male and female characters.

Name tags

If colours are being used to distinguish groups, have Group leaders prepare name tags of the assigned colour. Use bristol or poster board to cut out heart shapes. Punch a hole in the rounded parts of the heart and string a piece of matching coloured yarn or gimp through the holes to make a necklace. You may wish to use safety pins to attach to the child's clothing. To make an arm bracelet, place the holes on either side of the heart. Use a piece of elastic thread to make a wristband. To lengthen the life of the name tag, cover it with adhesive-backed clear plastic.

The tags are handed in to the Group leader at the end of each session. Encourage Group leaders to call each child by name as much as possible.

Closing celebration

A closing celebration has many useful purposes. Parents are given the opportunity to meet the Group leaders and teachers who led the program. Many parents like to know what their children are being taught in Christian education. A closing celebration provides the setting for them to meet with the leaders and to offer feedback on the curriculum. Leaders have the privilege of meeting and greeting the parents of the children they have had in their care.

This assembly is meant to be an informal gathering time for children, leaders, and parents, and not a polished performance by the children. Use this informal time to invite new families to continue to be a part of your worshiping community.

Some things to do in the celebration are:

- Sing the theme song and other favourites.
- Repeat the memory texts together.
- Have different groups repeat some of the memory texts.
- Review the stories by having a mini-drama.
- Display some of the crafts, art activities, door-hanging, etc.
- Show video clips of some of the activities (pre-recorded).
- Share a simple snack.
- Close with the "Go in Peace" blessing.

Loving God

Registration Form

Please complete this form and give it to the Group leader by______________________________.

Name of child____

Address ____

Telephone ____

Birth date ____
(month) (day) (year)

Last school grade completed ____

Known allergies or other medical concerns ____

____

Name of parent/primary caregiver____

Home telephone _________________________ Work telephone ___________________________

Emergency contact person ____

Emergency telephone ____

Does the child usually attend Sunday school? ______________________________________

If so, where? ____

Waiver of Responsibility

I give ____permission to participate in this
(child's name)

programme. The leaders will not be held responsible for injury, etc.

Parent/guardian signature ____

Date ____

Permission is granted to purchasers of this curriculum to photocopy this page for use with the Loving God *curriculum.*

Loving God Group Assignment Form

	NAME	AGE	GRADE	GROUP ASSIGNED	COMMENT

Permission is granted to purchasers of this curriculum to photocopy this page for use with the Loving God *curriculum.*

LOVING GOD *Attendance Form*

GROUP ______________________________

LEADERS ______________________________

NAME	SESSION 1	SESSION 2	SESSION 3	SESSION 4	SESSION 5	COMMENT
1.						
2.						
3.						
4.						
5.						
6.						
7.						
8.						
9.						
10.						
11						
12.						
13.						
14.						
15.						
16.						
17.						
18.						
19.						
20.						

Permission is granted to purchasers of this curriculum to photocopy this page for use with the Loving God *curriculum.*

Curriculum logo

Permission is granted to purchasers of this curriculum to photocopy this page for use with the Loving God *curriculum.*

Resources

Closing Blessing: "Go in Peace"

[*Stand together in a circle facing the centre.*]
Go in peace.
[*With your left hand make a sweeping motion away from your body.*]
Go in peace.
[*Keeping the left arm extended, make the same sweeping motion with your right arm.*]
May God's love circle round you.
[*Lower both arms, crossing and lifting both up in a circular motion above your head, then lowering your arms around your neighbour's back.*]
Wherever you go.
[*Sway to the left and to the right within your circle.*]

Notes:

1. Teach this to the whole group during Session 1. Use as a closing with smaller groups for the other sessions or with the entire group.
2. Group leaders can learn the song and the motions beforehand (see page 54).
3. Small groups could make up different motions if they wish.

Books

Although some of the books listed are secular books, the leader can easily relate them to the theme by asking such questions as: I wonder what this story tells us about God? I wonder how Jesus (or the biblical character of the session) would have handled the situation? However, usually the message of the story stands well by itself. Do not force a "Christian" message onto the story.

Session 1

Murray, Elspeth Campbell. *What Can I Say to You, God?* David and I Talk to God Series. Elgin, Ill.: David C. Cook, 1980. Any books from this series would be appropriate for any session for early childhood through grade 1. The books are prayers from the Psalms written so young children can understand them. Recommend this book for your church library if you do not already have it.

Caswell, Helen. *God's Love Is for Sharing.* Nashville, Tenn.: Abingdon Press, 1987. This book is for the youngest group and could be read for Sessions 1 and 5.

Session 2

Caswell, Helen. *I Can Talk to God.* Nashville: Abingdon Press, 1989.

Wilhelm, Hans. *A Cool Kid–Like Me.* New York, N.Y.: Crown Books for Young Readers, 1990. This story could be related to the way God listens to us.

Cynthia. *The Night There Was Thunder and Stuff.* Winfield, B.C.: Wood Lake Books, 1993. A good book on prayer for early childhood through grade 2.

Session 3

Foon, Dennis. *The Short Tree and the Bird That Could Not Sing.* Toronto, Ont.: Groundwood/Douglas and McIntyre, Firefly Books, Ltd., 1991. A book about a unique friendship, for early childhood through grade 1.

Fern, Eugene. *Pepito's Story*. (New York, N.Y.: Yarrow Press, 1991. A story about helping out a friend. This could be used for Session 5 also.

Polacco, Patricia. *Chicken Sunday*. (New York: Philomel Books, Putnam Publishing Group, 1992. A great story about friendship between generations. Good for Session 5 also.

Kasza, Keiko. *The Rat and the Tiger*. New York, N.Y.: Putnam Publishing Group, 1993. A story about the meaning of mutual respect in a friendship. For early childhood to grade 2.

Derby, Janice, illustrated by Joy Dunn Keenan. *Are You My Friend?* Scottdale, Pa.: Herald Press, 1993. Good for early childhood through grade 2.

Session 4

Lionni, Leo. *Tillie and the Wall*. Toronto, Ont.: Random House, Knopf Books for Young Readers, 1989. A good story for younger children.

Quinlan, Patricia. *Planting Seeds*. Toronto, Ont.: Annick Press, 1988. A good story about conflict management.

Session 5

Fox, Mem, illustrated by Julie Vivas. *Wilfrid Gordon McDonald Partridge*. Brooklyn, N.Y.: Kane Miller Books, 1985. A good book on friendship with seniors.

Fleming, Virginia. *Be Good to Eddie Lee*. New York: Philomel Books, Putnam Publishing Group, 1993. Eddie Lee is a Down's Syndrome child. This is an excellent story to illustrate the theme. Buy it for your church library.

Polacco, Patricia. *Mrs. Katz and Tush*. New York: Bantam Books, 1992.

General Books

Lehn, Cornelia. *Peace Be With You*. Newton, Kans.: Faith & Life Press, 1980. Good stories about Christians who lived out their faith. You can find a story for each day's theme in this excellent book.

Lehn, Cornelia. *I Heard Good News Today*. Newton, Kans.: Faith & Life Press, 1983. This book, too, contains many excellent and appropriate stories for these themes.

Lobel, Arnold. *Frog and Toad Are Friends*. New York: HarperCollins, 1970.

Lobel, Arnold. *Frog and Toad All Year*. New York: HarperCollins, 1976.

Lobel, Arnold. *Days with Frog and Toad*. New York: HarperCollins, 1979.

MacKenzie, Joy, with Joni Eareckson Tada. *Joni's Kids Activity Book*. Word Music, 1985. Games, songs, and activities for young children about friendship and loving others.

Meyer, Mary Clemens. *Walking with Jesus: Stories about real people who return good for evil*. Scottdale, Pa.: Herald Press, 1992. Excellent true stories that illustrate many of the themes for this curriculum. Highly recommended for church libraries.

Audiovisuals

"McGee and Me: Skate Expectations," Focus on the Family, 1989. A thirty-minute video.

Worship Resource

Introduction

Worship coordinator

The Worship coordinator is responsible to plan a meaningful worship experience through song, prayer, and Bible stories. Let the power of God's word, the music, and prayer speak to the children. Keep announcements to a minimum so as not to distract from the worship experience. Use your leadership gifts to show your love for God as you share that love with the children.

Bible stories

The biblical story is central to this curriculum. Pass it on to the children in an engaging and meaningful way. Use the dramas as one way to relate God's story of love for humanity. Arrange for a drama team or storyteller to present the Bible story for each session. Look for other creative ways to present the Bible stories that fit your group and setting.

The Bible stories are written in dramatic form for two or more characters. A different main character appears in each drama. David appears in both Sessions 3 and 5, and Abigail is part of both the Session 4 and Session 5 dramas.

Tell the children the theme of the day and the names of the characters in the drama. Trust their understanding of the story line to the power of the story itself. Through the dramas, the children will learn about the different ways that they can show their love to God and experience God's love for them.

Bible story presenters

Invite five people to form a drama team to practice and present each of the five dramas. Using a team will allow for consistency in character portrayal.

Meet with the Bible story presenters. Encourage the Bible story presenters to read both the Bible text and the dramas. Discuss the characters and how you will portray them. Make the characters come alive in your study of them so that the children can identify with them. Discuss the meaning of the theme in the texts and for their own lives. Pray together that God's love will be expressed in and through the story presenters.

Members of the drama team are encouraged to memorize their lines and present the dramas with enthusiasm and meaning. It is very important that the dramas are well presented because they form the basis for the response activities that follow.

Costuming

Find simple clothing to represent life in Bible times. Brown bathrobes, shepherds' costumes used in Christmas pageants, and leather thongs or sandals help children get into the story in a visual way.

Staging

Some simple staging suggestions are given for each session. Add to and adapt these suggestions to fit your setting for the dramas and your dramatic skills.

Format

The Bible story dramas are presented as part of Worship for children from kindergarten through grade 8 (see Schedule, pages 20-22). After opening announcements and group singing, have someone introduce the theme of the day to the children. Explain that the stories come from the Old Testament in the books of Samuel and that these stories tell how people showed their love for God in different ways. Give a little background about the setting and time of these stories. Check a Bible commentary or dictionary for such information.

Music

Appropriate music including the theme song, "Love the Lord Your God," is suggested for each worship time. The songs are printed on pages 54-60. If you are not comfortable leading the music, enlist the help of a musician. If possible, use instruments, junior youth, or a music team to help you in your music leadership. As you share your gift of music, enjoy yourself!

Have a good grasp of the songs that you wish the children to sing. Begin the sessions with familiar songs that are fun and celebrative. The music can draw children into praise and worship of God.

Dismissal

After Worship, the children will move to their first rotation activity where they will have the opportunity to respond to the story through games, prayer, discussion, crafts, and art. Make sure each Group leader knows the order of the rotation to Talk and Move, Pray and Learn, and Make and Take. The junior youth group will move to its own session at this time. See Schedule, pages 20-22, for session plans.

If your program is designed for the individual graded approach (pages 22-23), the children will go to their graded classrooms at this time.

Session plans for Worship

Session 1

Hannah

Theme: Loving God by Praying
Bible Text: 1 Samuel 1:1—2:1-11
Story Focus: Hannah's love for God was demonstrated in her prayer life. She trusted that God would answer her prayer. She fulfilled her promise to God when she took Samuel to the temple to live with Eli.
Faith Focus: We show that we love God when we talk to God. We trust that God will hear and answer us when we pray.

Anticipated Outcomes

1. Children will be introduced to Hannah, a character from the Old Testament.
2. Children will learn how Hannah expressed her love to God by talking to God and trusting that God would answer her prayer.

Worship

Greet everyone and thank them for participating in *Loving God.* Invite them to make a commitment to attend and participate in the entire *Loving God* programme.

Make any necessary announcements. Sings songs on pages 54-60 and other favourites as the children gather. Introduce the theme song, "Love the Lord Your God," page 54. Pray, asking God to be present and bless your time of worship together.

Characters

Hannah: A woman (late twenties) who desperately wants to have a baby but has been unable to get pregnant for some time. She is passionate and articulate in her prayers.

Peninnah: A woman in her mid-thirties. She is a jealous rival to Hannah. Peninnah seems to rejoice in Hannah's misfortune.

Elkanah: Husband to Hannah and Peninnah. Elkanah is portrayed here as an uncomplicated person who enjoys life, especially eating!

Eli: An older man who is the priest of the temple. He takes the concerns of all his people to heart.

Setting
Scene 1: At the temple stairs.
Scene 2: The nursery at the home of Hannah and Elkanah.

Staging suggestions
If the play is to be performed in a church sanctuary, use the steps that go to the pulpit as the place where Hannah is waiting. For Scene 2, use representational props to help give the impression of a small boy's room (cot, toys, etc.).

Props
Scene 1: basket for Hannah, filled with food items; apple or other food for Elkanah to munch on
Scene 2: toys scattered on the floor

Scene 1

Peninnah: [*At the temple stairs*] What's wrong, Hannah? You should be in the temple.
Hannah: I thought I would wait here.
Peninnah: You have a lot of nerve. I would think you'd stay in the temple and beg God to hear you. You know God is angry with you.
Hannah: God isn't angry with me.
Peninnah: Then why doesn't God give you any children?
Hannah: I don't know.
Peninnah: You must have done something to anger God. God is punishing you. All the rest of us have plenty of children. You are the only one who doesn't.
Hannah: I know that, Peninnah. Right now your children are wondering where their mother is, so why don't you go find them?
Peninnah: You can try to get rid of me if you want to, Hannah. But you know as well as I do that every time we come to the temple, you are the only one who leaves without God's blessing. You must have some evil in you that you are not admitting. Otherwise God would give you a child.
Hannah: Please, Peninnah, just leave me alone [*Starting to cry*].
Peninnah: Sure, you can sulk out here, but I don't think that will please God either. [*Peninnah exits to the temple. Enter Elkanah.*]
Elkanah: Hannah, why are you crying?
Hannah: Because of what Peninnah said to me.
Elkanah: Ignore her.
Hannah: Maybe Peninnah's right. I've done something wrong, and I'll never give you a child.
Elkanah: Hannah, don't be so sad. This is a time for celebration!
Hannah: I want to give you something to celebrate about, Elkanah.
Elkanah: I know you love me, Hannah. But aren't you glad there aren't any more little Elkanahs running around?
Hannah: What do you mean?
Elkanah: Imagine all the laundry, all the mending [*Munching on a chicken leg*], all the food you would have to prepare? Don't I make up for ten children?

Hannah: [*Laughing through her tears*] Elkanah, believe it or not, I could handle ten more like you.
Elkanah: That's better, Hannah. I like to see you laugh. Now come inside the temple with me.
Hannah: Elkanah, I would like to wait here a little longer. My heart is still sad. I'm not ready to celebrate with the others.
Elkanah: As you wish, Hannah. But please come in soon.
Hannah: Yes, Elkanah. [*Elkanah exits to the inside of the temple.*]
[*Sounds from the celebration are heard during Hannah's prayer.*]
Hannah: Oh Lord, how empty I feel. See how miserable I am. I feel so alone. Please God, do not forget me, your servant. Remember me and give me a child. If you will remember me and give me a child, I will give my child to your service, to serve you and your people in the temple. O Lord, hear my prayer.
Eli: Hannah, why do you not come into the temple?
Hannah: [*Stands up abruptly, almost knocks her basket over.*]
Eli: So that is why you don't want to join the others. You are drunk.
Hannah: No, Eli.
Eli: Well, you are acting very strange. I am sure you were talking to yourself when I found you here.
Hannah: You are a person who loves God. You know that sometimes we need to be alone to pour out our souls to the Lord.
Eli: Were you pouring out your soul to the Lord?
Hannah: Yes, Eli. I am very anxious and worried.
Eli: And what have you asked of the Lord?
Hannah: I have asked for a child.
Eli: Go in peace. May the God of Israel answer your prayer.
Hannah: Thank you, Eli.
Eli: Now, let's go inside with the others, Hannah, before your husband eats all the food!
[*Eli and Hannah exit to the temple.*]

Scene 2: Transition Scene
[*Actors take the props from the first scene and transform the temple into a bedroom/nursery. Hannah and Elkanah bring in a baby and place it in the crib. A servant rushes through the audience shouting: "It's a boy! Hannah had a baby boy!" The actors then remove the baby things. To indicate that time has passed, the actors place some little boy's toys around the room.*]

Scene 2
[*Hannah's bedroom/nursery, three years later; Hannah is picking up toys and trying to put the room in order. Enter Elkanah, eating.*]
Elkanah: Hannah! Hannah!
Hannah: [*Enters, breathless*] Yes, Elkanah?
Elkanah: We're ready to go to the temple. Where's Samuel?
Hannah: Oh, the servant is getting him dressed, Elkanah. I have tried to keep him looking nice, but he keeps getting into something, and I have to start all over!
Elkanah: He's a normal boy, my dear.
Hannah: I know and I love him dearly. I just wish he would stand still for a minute or two.
Elkanah: Well, let's go. Are you sure you are ready for this, Hannah?

Hannah: Yes, Elkanah. I prayed for this child, and the Lord granted my request. I promised that Samuel would serve God in the temple. It is time that I kept my part of the promise. It is time for Samuel to leave us. Eli will take good care of him, and Samuel will learn to serve the Lord. I am privileged to be a mother to such a son.

Elkanah: And I am privileged to have such a wife. [*They hear a crash.*] Now come, my dear, let's go before Samuel gets into something else! [*He rushes to get Samuel.*]

Hannah: [*Kneels by her bed and looks heavenward*] My heart rejoices in you, Lord. I am strengthened by you. You have raised me from the dust; you have listened to me in my need. I am so very thankful for my son.

Elkanah: [*Off-stage, the sound of another crash and Elkanah's stricken voice*] HANNAH!

Hannah: [*Glancing heavenward before she exits, running*] Well, most of the time.

"Hannah," written and owned by Kathleen Cleland Moyer. Adapted and used by permission of the author. Permission is granted to those who purchase this resource to photocopy for use only as part of the *Loving God* curriculum.

Dismissal

Without discussing the story, dismiss the children to their activities where they will respond to the story in an appropriate way. See Schedule, pages 20-22, for the activity plan.

Session 2

Samuel

Theme: Loving God by Listening
Bible Text: 1 Samuel 2:18-21, 26; 3:1-21
Story Focus: When Samuel realized that God was calling to him, he responded by listening to God's voice.
Faith Focus: We show that we love God when we listen for God's voice and respond.

Anticipated Outcomes

1. Children will be introduced to Samuel, a character from the Old Testament.
2. Children will learn how Samuel expressed his love for God by listening for, and responding to, God's voice.

Worship

Make any necessary announcements. Sing songs from pages 54-60. Continue learning the theme song, "Love the Lord Your God." Pray, asking God's presence and blessing on the activities of the day.

Characters

Samuel: A typical teenager with lots of energy and charm. He is perhaps a bit too sure of himself at times.
Eli: Samuel's guardian and the high priest. He is in his early seventies and scolds Samuel frequently, but always affectionately.
Voice: Offstage. An adult voice.

Setting

Inside the temple and at Eli's sleeping quarters.

Staging suggestions

Samuel could sleep in a sleeping bag on a table that is high enough for everyone to see him. Eli could have a cot set up in an area to the left of the altar. There could be a makeshift curtain set up between the two areas to indicate the cot is in another room, or Samuel could mime going through a door or a curtain every time he enters and exits Eli's room.

Props
Candles (preferably on a candelabrum); large wooden matches; sleeping bags; pillows

Scene 1

Eli: [*Having a hard time striking a match due to poor eyesight—enter Samuel*] Here, Samuel...you need to practice. You light the temple candles.

Samuel: Sure. [*He lights them without a problem, in a cocky manner.*] Anything else I can do?

Eli: Yes, don't get proud. Just because I'm old and can't see as well as I once did doesn't mean I don't see what's inside people.

Samuel: I know, Eli. [*Mimics Eli*] I have a lot to learn.

Eli: [*Laughing*] Yes, you do! And you need to get to bed so that you are able to learn more tomorrow.

Samuel: Eli, it's early.

Eli: The days are coming that I will no longer be with you, Samuel. You have a lot to learn about the temple. Now get to bed.

Samuel: Why can't I learn it now, Eli? I don't learn much when I'm asleep.

Eli: Waking or sleeping, a person of God is always waiting to hear the word of the Lord.

Samuel: But God hasn't talked to anyone in ages. We should stay awake and maybe God would tell us why.

Eli: We should sleep.

Samuel: Well, I will sleep here. If God is going to speak, at least I will be here in the temple.

Eli: But God can speak anywhere.

Samuel: I know, Eli, but I want to stay here, next to the ark of God.

Eli: As you wish, Samuel. I am tired, and I don't think it matters where you sleep as long as you are ready for a full day of instruction tomorrow. Now say your prayers to the Lord. May God bless your dreams.

Samuel: Good night, Eli.

[*Eli goes to his room and blows out the candle. Samuel lies down in front of the ark in the temple. Allow for a moment of silence as Samuel falls asleep.*]

Voice: Samuel! Samuel!

Samuel: [*Sits up*] Eli? [*He rushes to Eli's room.*] Here I am, Eli. Can I do something for you?

Eli: [*Waking, grumpily*] Yes. You can do something for me. Don't bother me and get back to bed.

Samuel: But you called me.

Eli: I did not call, Samuel. Now get back to bed.

[*Samuel and Eli resume sleeping positions.*]

Voice: Samuel! Samuel!

[*Samuel wakes up again, puzzled.*]

Samuel: [*Tentatively*] Eli? [*He can't wake Eli this time, so he shakes him*] Eli, Eli!

Eli: whhhwhatwhy...Samuel! What on earth are you doing?

Samuel: You called me again.

Eli: Samuel, I am not so old that I forget if I am awake or asleep, and I [*He yawns*] was blissfully asleep. Now go back to bed and let an old man rest.

Samuel: But I heard you call.

Eli: Samuel, you are hearing things. Now get back to bed.

Samuel: But...

Eli: Samuel, I did not call you. But if I did, I would shout this message at the top of my lungs.

Samuel: What's that?

Eli: [*In a big voice*] GET TO SLEEP!

Samuel: Okay, Eli.

[*Samuel and Eli resume sleeping positions.*]

Voice: SAMUEL, SAMUEL!

Samuel: [*Sits up*] Oh, no! Either Eli's going crazy or I am.

Samuel: Eli? [*He walks tentatively to Eli's room.*] Eli?

[*Eli is snoring loudly.*]

Samuel: Eli, wake up. Eli, please.

Eli: Huh?

Samuel: Guess who?

Eli: I called you again?

Samuel: Yes.

Eli: Samuel, are you trying to get me angry?

Samuel: No, Eli. I'm trying to figure out if one of us is crazy.

Eli: Well, that's easy. I'm sleeping; it's nighttime. That's not crazy. You're crashing in here every few minutes telling me I'm talking to you...now that's crazy.

Samuel: I heard someone call me. Who else could it be?

Eli: No one else. That's my point.

Samuel: As God lives, I heard my name called.

Eli: Now son.... Hey! Wait a minute! I've been an old fool.

Samuel: What do you mean?

Eli: It was the Lord! You heard the Lord calling your name.

Samuel: The Lord was calling me?

Eli: I can't believe I didn't think of it earlier, Samuel. Of course, God was speaking to you.

Samuel: God?!

Eli: Yes.

Samuel: But God should be speaking to you. You are the priest. I'm too young.

Eli: God speaks to the young, too, Samuel.

Samuel: Well, what do I do?

Eli: You listen to God.

Samuel: But what if I don't understand?

Eli: You just listen.

Samuel: Just listen.

[*Goes back to his room.*]

Voice: Samuel!

Samuel: [*Rising*] Speak, Lord. I am your servant, and I am listening.

"Samuel," written and owned by Kathleen Cleland Moyer. Adapted and used by permission of the author. Permission is granted to those who purchase this resource to photocopy for use only as part of the *Loving God* curriculum.

Dismissal

Dismiss the groups to their response activities following the rotation pattern or plan you have made. See Schedule, pages 20-22.

Session 3

Jonathan

Theme: Loving God by Loving Others
Bible Text: 1 Samuel 20:1-42
Bible Background: 1 Samuel 18 and 19
Story Focus: Jonathan risked his life for his best friend, David, though it meant danger for him.
Faith Focus: We show that we love God when we are a true friend.

Anticipated Outcomes

1. Children will be introduced to Jonathan and his close friend, David, both characters from the Old Testament.
2. Children will learn how Jonathan expressed his love to God by being a true friend.

Worship

Make any necessary announcements. Sing songs on pages 54-60. Include other favourites that the children know well. Sing your theme song, "Love the Lord Your God." Pray that everyone gathered may listen to the word of God as presented through the Bible story drama.

Characters

King Saul: A powerful man in his fifties, who is afraid that he is losing his power. He has a hard time controlling his anger against David who is his son's best friend.
Jonathan: Saul's son and David's best friend. He is in his early twenties.
David: A young man of modest background who is popular with the people and is unintentionally seen as a threat to the king.
Servant: The king's servant.

Setting

Scenes 1 and 3: At the palace

Scenes 2 and 4: In a field

Staging suggestions
Palace: The king should be at centre stage with the table angled to his right. The window can be mimed or an actual window in the sanctuary can be used. Field: There should be a few trees as props.

Props
Scene 1: a spear for the king
Scene 3: a tablecloth and dishes

Scene 1
[*At the palace. Saul sits on his throne, attended by his servant. There is the sound of people singing, cheering, and rejoicing outside the palace.*]

Saul: [*To his servant*] What is it? What is going on?

Servant: [*Goes to the window to look out. Returns and speaks excitedly*] David has returned, your majesty! The people are celebrating because David has returned.

Saul: And who is this David? The son of some Bethlehemite...a shepherd...why, the people are treating him like a king!

Servant: He has won a great battle, sir.

Saul: And haven't I?

Servant: Yes, of course, but the people say the Lord is with David.

Saul: David, the shepherd! He is nothing but an opportunist. My son gives him his robe, his bow, and his armor. For what? So that he can come back and make fun of us. Go get my son, Jonathan. Maybe now he will see David for what he really is.

Servant: Yes, your majesty. But I think Jonathan may be out welcoming David back, too.

Saul: GO GET HIM!

Servant: Right away, your majesty!
[*Exit Servant. The sound rises from outside, while Saul paces in anger. The servant brings Jonathan. David is with him. They are laughing about something. David slaps Jonathan affectionately on the back and runs off.*]

Jonathan: You should see all the people out there, father. David has brought great honour to our people.

Saul: David has disgraced us! Don't you see that, Jonathan? You are the king's son. Instead, that son of a shepherd is taking glory away from us!

Jonathan: Father, David is our friend. He is my friend.

Saul: He uses you so he can get popular with the people. He acts as if he deserves being popular. What he deserves is death!

Jonathan: He serves us. He serves God. He can't help it if the people are happy with his victories.

Saul: The people used to be happy with my victories. Now they don't even pay attention. [*There is a swell of noise from outside*] David shall be killed!

Jonathan: Father, you don't mean that. David risked his life to face Goliath for you and for the people of Israel. You were happy then. How can you kill a person who has risked his life to serve you? Our God does not allow us to kill innocent people.

Saul: Jonathan. I don't understand you. You stand up for your rival. I am finally seeing that you have spoken wisely. David shall not be put to death. Now go and join in the foolishness.

[*Jonathan exits. Saul calls to his servant.*]

Saul: Servant, stand and wait outside David's house. He will be alone in the morning. When he leaves his house, you must kill him.

Servant: As you wish, your majesty. [*Servant exits.*]

Scene 2

[*In a field. David is behind a tree. Jonathan is walking toward the palace.*]

David: [*In a stage whisper*] Jonathan!

Jonathan: [*Looks around*] Who is it? [*Sees David*] David!

David: Jonathan, are you alone?

Jonathan: Yes, David. What are you doing?

David: Jonathan, I need to talk to you.

Jonathan: Come on. No one can see us here.

[*They sit in front of the tree.*]

David: Jonathan, what have I done? What is my sin against your father that he tries to kill me?

Jonathan: David, I've talked to him. He says he won't harm you.

David: I just escaped his spear twice in the last few days.

Jonathan: David, he would tell me if he were going to kill you. He tells me everything.

David: Jonathan, he doesn't want to tell you this. I swear to you. He has his men after me. I feel as if death is chasing me.

Jonathan: It is hard to believe my father is capable of such evil.

David: Do you think I am lying and your father is telling the truth?

Jonathan: You are a true friend, David. I trust you as I trust myself. It is just difficult to accept that my father has such evil plans.

David: Why don't we try something that will test his true feelings?

Jonathan: What can I do? If what you are saying is true, then my father is lying to me.

David: I have an idea. I will not come to the king's dinner table tomorrow, or the next day, or the next day. See what your father does. If he gets angry because I am not there, we will know that he wants to see me dead.

Jonathan: I will do as you ask, David. But you realize, if my father is as angry as you think, he will expect me to be your sworn enemy.

David: I know, Jonathan.

Jonathan: And if my father tries to kill you, an innocent man, you could also see me as your enemy.

David: I will never do that, Jonathan. You are a friend like no other. You risk being dishonoured by your father for my sake; you risk your life to save mine. I will not betray our friendship.

Jonathan: The Lord has brought us together in friendship. I could not desert you any more than I could my own soul. Wait for me behind those stones, David. And in three days, I will tell you the truth about my father.

Scene 3

[*In the palace. Jonathan and Servant. The Servant sets the table for the king's meal.*]

Jonathan: [*To servant*] Tell me, is the table set for all of us?

Servant: David did not come to the table last night, sir. I thought it better not to remind your father of his absence.

Jonathan: He said nothing to us last night when he realized David was not there. Did he say something to you?

Servant: No, my lord. But he may have been holding his temper.

Jonathan: You must do as I say. Set the table for David. He may surprise us and come.

Servant: As you wish.
[*Enter Saul. Saul and Jonathan take their places at the table. David's place is obviously empty.*]

Saul: [*To the servant*] Has David, the son of Jesse, come yet?

Servant: No, your highness.

Saul: [*To Jonathan*] Why has David not come to the meal either yesterday or today?

Jonathan: David asked me, with all respect, to be excused so that he could go to the temple with his family. It is for this reason that he has not come to the king's table.

Saul: How dare he turn down an invitation from the king! And how dare you allow him to make fun of us!

Jonathan: I thought it would do no harm.

Saul: You thought that disobeying me would do no harm? How dare you! You choose to defend a son of a shepherd instead of your own father, the king!

Jonathan: David doesn't want to harm you.

Saul: What shame you bring on us, Jonathan! You give up your kingdom to stand up for this worthless shepherd boy! Don't you see how he is using you! As long as he lives, you will never be able to be the king!

Jonathan: David is my friend.

Saul: And you are a fool. Act like a man. Stand up for yourself. Don't let David rob you of your inheritance to be king after me. If you are too much of a coward to defend yourself, I will do it. Get David and bring him here. He shall die.

Jonathan: Why should he be put to death? What has he done?

Saul: You continue to talk back to me! You try to take away my power as the king. You are not a son to me, but a traitor.

Jonathan: Father!

Saul: Do not call me that. [*He pulls out his spear and throws it at David's empty seat.*] If you will not bring him to me, I will find him myself.
[*Saul exits in a rage. Jonathan exits, running.*]

Scene 4

Jonathan: [*In the field*] David. David. I am alone. You can come out.

David: Jonathan! I am so tired from waiting. What happened?

Jonathan: You were right. Some evil has taken hold of my father, and he wants to kill you. I have to hurry before he finds me. You must disappear and hide.

David: Jonathan, God has made you like a brother to me. Brothers are not meant to be separated.

Jonathan: While my father lives, it is too dangerous to be friends.

David: Danger or not, Jonathan, we will be friends. Go in peace.

Jonathan: Go in peace.

"Jonathan," written and owned by Kathleen Cleland Moyer. Adapted and used by permission of the author. Permission is granted to those who purchase this resource to photocopy for use only as part of the *Loving God* curriculum.

Dismissal

Dismiss the groups to their response activities. Follow the activity rotation plan or the schedule you have set up. See Schedule, pages 20-22.

Session 4

Abigail

Theme: Loving God by Making Peace
Bible Text: 1 Samuel 25:1-38
Story Focus: Abigail demonstrated creative thinking skills and action in order to keep peace between two enemies, Nabal and David.
Faith Focus: We show that we love God when we solve our problems in peaceful ways.

Anticipated Outcomes

1. Children will be introduced to Abigail, a character from the Old Testament.
2. Children will learn how Abigail expressed her love to God by being a peacemaker.

Worship

Make necessary announcements. Sing favourite songs, your theme song, and other songs from pages 54-60. Introduce the Bible drama for this session.

Characters
Abigail: A young woman who is strong and fair-minded.
Servant: A fourteen-year-old girl who idolizes Abigail as much as she despises Abigail's husband.
Nabal: A bad-tempered man who is insensitive and dull.
Shepherd: A twenty-year-old male servant who has overcome his fear of talking directly to Abigail.
David: The leader of the army, known for being tough but fair.
Soldiers: Young men with David. One soldier has a speaking part.

Setting
Scene 1: Abigail and Nabal's dining tent
Scene 2: A field

Props
Scene 1: Table laden with food, dishes in preparation for a feast; sheep shears
Scene 2: Sacks filled with food items; a spear

Scene 1

Servant: Abigail, oh Abigail. You have got to talk to your husband. He's yelling and cursing at all the servants. We are trying to get everything ready for the feast. Please, Abigail, we can only take so much from him.

Abigail: I would, my dear, if it would do any good. But Nabal is bad tempered, and nothing I say to him changes that.

Servant: How can you be married to such a man? You are as sweet as he is sour. You are as beautiful as he is homely. You are as intelligent as he is stu.... [*Enter Nabal, shears in hand.*]

Abigail: Hush. Here's Nabal.

Servant: [*Rushes behind Abigail and whispers in her ear*] Did he hear me, Abigail? I fear he would shear me instead of the sheep if he heard me!

Abigail: I don't think he did. [*She gives the servant a gentle push*] Now, just walk quietly away. [*Servant exits rushing past Nabal in utter terror.*]

Nabal: What is that silly girl going on about?

Abigail: Nothing, my dear. The servants are just excited because of the feast.

Nabal: Of course they are excited. They don't have to pay for it. I do. Just thinking of all those shepherds eating my prize calves makes me lose my appetite!

Abigail: If it weren't for the shepherds, we couldn't afford prize calves, Nabal.

Nabal: Now don't you start, Abigail. Your father told me you would be a quiet, submissive wife.

Abigail: You told my father you would be a thoughtful and generous husband.

Nabal: There you go again, Abigail. I forbid you to talk to me in that tone of voice! I am the man of the house...and I will make any sarcastic remarks there are to be made. [*Nabal exits, tripping over his shears. Enter the Male Servant.*]

Shepherd: Ma'am, may I have a word with you.

Abigail: If it is about my husband, no. I can't help you.

Shepherd: But, ma'am, your husband has done something that will cause all of us great harm.

Abigail: I assure you, you will all have plenty to eat at the feast even if he rants and raves.

Shepherd: We are all used to his nature. We are no longer insulted when he hurls abuse and insults.

Abigail: Then what has he done?

Shepherd: He has chosen to insult soldiers from David's army who asked to join us for the feast.

Abigail: He insulted David!

Shepherd: For months David and his soldiers have protected us from attack and allowed us to continue watching our sheep. It is unthinkable that your husband should not welcome them to the feast.

Abigail: And what happens when so great a man as David is insulted in this way?

Shepherd: David will seek revenge. He will be gathering the army together now. I don't think they will spare any of us.

Abigail: They will kill you all because of my husband's bad temper?
Shepherd: I am afraid so, my lady.
Abigail: Then I shall ask my husband to apologize!
Shepherd: I do not wish to belittle your power of persuasion, my lady, but I have never known your husband to apologize.
Abigail: Of course, you are right. Then what are we to do? [*They both think for a few moments.*] I know. I could apologize for my husband.
Shepherd: But you are a woman!
Abigail: They say that David is a fair man who would not harm a woman.
Shepherd: But it might not work. They might be all ready to attack. We should travel quickly.
Abigail: You are right. Do you think you could get me some things that are ready for the feast without my husband seeing you?
Shepherd: I will find someone to distract him. What things do you want?
Abigail: We will need some gifts to prove to David that we are sincere in our apology. Get all the loaves of bread that are ready for the feast. I think there are two hundred. Bring five sheep, a hundred clusters of raisins, and all the cakes. Pack them on the donkeys. We will travel to David's camp as quickly as we can.

Scene 2

Shepherd: [*In the field*] There he is. There's David. Oh my lady, it looks as if he is ready for battle.
Abigail: Well, then, we made it here just in time. [*She runs in front of David, and falls before him, with her face to the ground.*]
David: Who is this? [*The men around David draw their spears.*]
Abigail: Oh, my lord, please listen to me. I am sorry that my husband, Nabal, insulted you. You have a right to be angry, but I pray of you to listen to my humble words.
David: You are the wife of that bad-tempered Nabal? I have guarded all your husband's property so that nothing happened to any of his servants or his animals, and he has disgraced me. He has returned evil for good.
Abigail: I know, my lord. But please pay no attention to a foolish man who does not consult with the God of Israel. I did not know about your request to join us until after your men had been insulted by my husband. Pray forgive us. Though you have been wronged, I pray that the God of Israel will stop you from taking revenge with your own hand.
David: You speak very eloquently.
Abigail: I not only bring you words. I pray that you and your men will accept this food that we prepared for our feast. [*Abigail's servant brings bundles of food.*]
Soldier: Do not be swayed by a woman, David. She is trying to buy us off. We are entitled to avenge Nabal.
David: The Lord, the God of Israel, will take revenge if it is necessary. [*He bends down, takes Abigail's hand, and raises her to her feet.*] My lady, blessed by the Lord God of Israel, who sent you this day to meet me. Blessed be your beautiful way of making peace.
Abigail: I was afraid, but your words have soothed me.
David: Go in peace to your house. I have listened to you, and I promise that I will not bring any harm to you or to your household.

Abigail: [*As she turns to leave*] I believe them, David, when they say you will one day be king of Israel.

David: And I believe them, my lady, when they say that strength and dignity make a woman truly beautiful. [*Exit Abigail.*]

"Abigail," written and owned by Kathleen Cleland Moyer. Adapted and used by permission of the author. Permission is granted to those who purchase this resource to photocopy for use only as part of the *Loving God* curriculum.

Dismissal

Dismiss the groups to their response activities. Follow the Schedule, pages 20-22, or the plan you have made.

Session 5

David

Theme: Loving God by Showing Kindness
Bible Text: 2 Samuel 4:4; 9:1-13
Story Focus: David showed kindness and brought Mephibosheth, Jonathan's son, into his home.
Faith Focus: We show that we love God when we are kind, just, and generous.

Anticipated Outcomes

1. Children will be introduced to David, a character from the Old Testament.
2. Children will learn how David expressed his love to God by being kind, just, and generous to Mephibosheth.

Worship

Sing all the favourite songs from your time together. Include the theme song. Pray together, thanking God for being present with you during your sessions and inviting the children to choose to follow God's way and to live a life that shows their love for God.

Characters

Abigail: Same as in Session 4, but she is now David's wife.
David: The king
Servant: A servant of King David
Mephibosheth: Jonathan's son who was injured as a baby and now walks with a limp.
Ziba: A servant of Mephibosheth

Setting
Scenes 1 and 2: the palace

Stage suggestions
The throne should be less ornate and imposing than the one used for King Saul.

Props
A wrapped gift (possibly in cloth)

Scene 1
[*Abigail enters running, carrying a gift.*]
David: Abigail, where are you off to?
Abigail: Oh, sorry, my King. I didn't see you. I just finished making this gift for my friend, Anaheim.
David: She is a good friend to you, Abigail.
Abigail: She is like a sister, my lord.
David: God gave me a friend like that, but he was killed by the Philistines.
Abigail: You mean Jonathan?
David: Yes, Abigail. Jonathan was a friend like no other. Even though it was his birthright, Jonathan's greatest wish for me was to be king, but he didn't live to see it.
Abigail: It is better to have had such a friend, even if you lose your friend, than never to understand what friendship means.
David: I'm not sure. I thought my heart would turn to stone when I heard that Jonathan was killed.
Abigail: One's heart does not turn to stone from loving, my lord, only from not loving.
David: You are a wise woman, Abigail.
Abigail: It is not so much wisdom as experience, my lord. They say that my husband Nabal's heart was so cold and hard that it died within him.
David: You are still wise, Abigail...and loving, but your friend may not think so if you don't get the gift to her.
Abigail: Oh, yes, I must run. Do not grieve so much for Jonathan. He would not want you to be so sad. [*Abigail exits. David rings bell for his servant. Enter servant.*]
David: Servant, is there anyone left of the house of Saul that I may show kindness for Jonathan's sake?
Servant: No one of any importance, my lord.
David: What does that mean?
Servant: Well, I've heard there is one person, but I hardly think you would be interested in him.
David: Who is this person?
Servant: He is Jonathan's son, my lord.
David: Jonathan's son! Bring him to me immediately.
Servant: But, my lord, he is crippled. He was injured as a young child and has been lame ever since.
David: What difference does that make? Is not our Lord the Lord of all? I had no idea that Jonathan's son was alive. Bring him to me immediately!
Servant: It is not our custom to bring the lame to the king.
David: It is also not our custom to have servants advise the king. Bring him.
Servant: As you wish, my lord.

Scene 2

[*Enter Ziba and Mephibosheth.*]

Ziba: The king told us to wait here, my son. Are you comfortable?

Mephibosheth: Yes, Ziba. But I am frightened.

Ziba: Of King David?

Mephibosheth: My grandfather Saul hated David. He tried many times to kill him. But David never tried to harm him.

Ziba: Then we have nothing to fear.

Mephibosheth: But David was not king then. Maybe now he will decide to seek revenge.

Ziba: [*He sees David*] Well, we will soon find out. [*Enter David. Mephibosheth falls on his face before David.*]

David: You are Jonathan's son!

Mephibosheth: I am Mephibosheth. I am your servant.

David: [*Reaches down and raises Mephibosheth to this feet*] Do not fear. I called you here so that I may show you kindness.

Mephibosheth: It would be a great honour, my lord, if I could serve you in the palace. Since my father and grandfather have died, we are poor. I cannot use my legs, but I am very capable in many ways.

David: Of course you shall stay here. But you will not be my servant. You will be as my son. You will sit at my table with the rest of my sons.

Mephibosheth: My lord!

Ziba: That is most generous, my lord. But he is lame. How can he sit at the King's table?

David: The Lord of Israel welcomes all to the table. Why should I refuse anyone?

Mephibosheth: No one has ever treated me this way, my lord.

David: You are Jonathan's son. I can never repay him for his kindness to me, but I can help you.

Mephibosheth: Blessed by King David who shows his people the way of kindness.

David: It is the Lord of Israel who has showed us kindness. [*David puts his arm around Mephibosheth's shoulders.*] Now let's see if we can get someone to show us some food! [*They exit.*]

"David," written and owned by Kathleen Cleland Moyer. Adapted and used by permission of the author. Permission is granted to those who purchase this resource to photocopy for use only as part of the *Loving God* curriculum.

Dismissal

Thank the Bible story presenters for their gift of storytelling. Make any final announcements. Dismiss the groups to their response activities.

Songs

The theme song, "Love the Lord Your God," can be sung each session to help develop the overall theme and memory work. The song "Lord, Listen to your Children Praying" is used in the Pray and Learn Resource each session You will want to check with the leader of this section as to whether it will be taught there or during the Worship Teach "Go in Peace" as a closing blessing with the whole group. The motions are found on page 30. Music by Natalie Sleeth for "Go Now in Peace" is found in *Becoming God's Peacemakers*, Living Stones Collection (Newton, Kans. Faith & Life Press, pp. 145-147) and *Hymnal: A Worship Book* (Elgin, Ill.: Brethren Press; Newton, Kans.: Faith & Life Press; Scottdale, Penn.: Mennonite Publishing House, p. 429).

This song may be sung as a three-part round with second and third groups entering at respective numbers.

Celebrate God's Love

Words and Music: Mark Sedio. Copyright © 1988 Mark Sedio. All rights reserved. Used by permission.

Here I Am, Lord

*1. I, the Lord of sea and sky,
I have heard my people cry.
All who dwell in dark and sin my hand will save.
I who made the stars of night,
I will make their darkness bright.
Who will bear my light to them?
Whom shall I send?
(Refrain)

2. I, the Lord of snow and rain,
I have borne my people's pain.
I have wept for love of them.
They turn away.
I will break their hearts of stone,
give them hearts for love alone.
I will speak my word to them.
Whom shall I send?
(Refrain)

3. I, the Lord of wind and flame,
I will tend the poor and lame.
I will set a feast for them.
My hand will save.
Finest bread I will provide,
till their hearts be satisfied.
I will give my life to them.
Whom shall I send?
(Refrain)

© 1981, Daniel L. Schutte and New Dawn Music. P.O. Box 13248, Portland, OR 97213-0248. All rights reserved. Used with permission.

*See *Hymnal Accompaniment Handbook,* page 395, (Brethren Press, Elgin, IL; Faith & Life Press, Newton, KS; and Mennonite Publishing House, Scottdale, PA).

Lord, Listen to Your Children Praying

Copyright © 1973 by Hope Publishing Co., Carol Stream, IL 60188. All rights reserved. Used by permission.

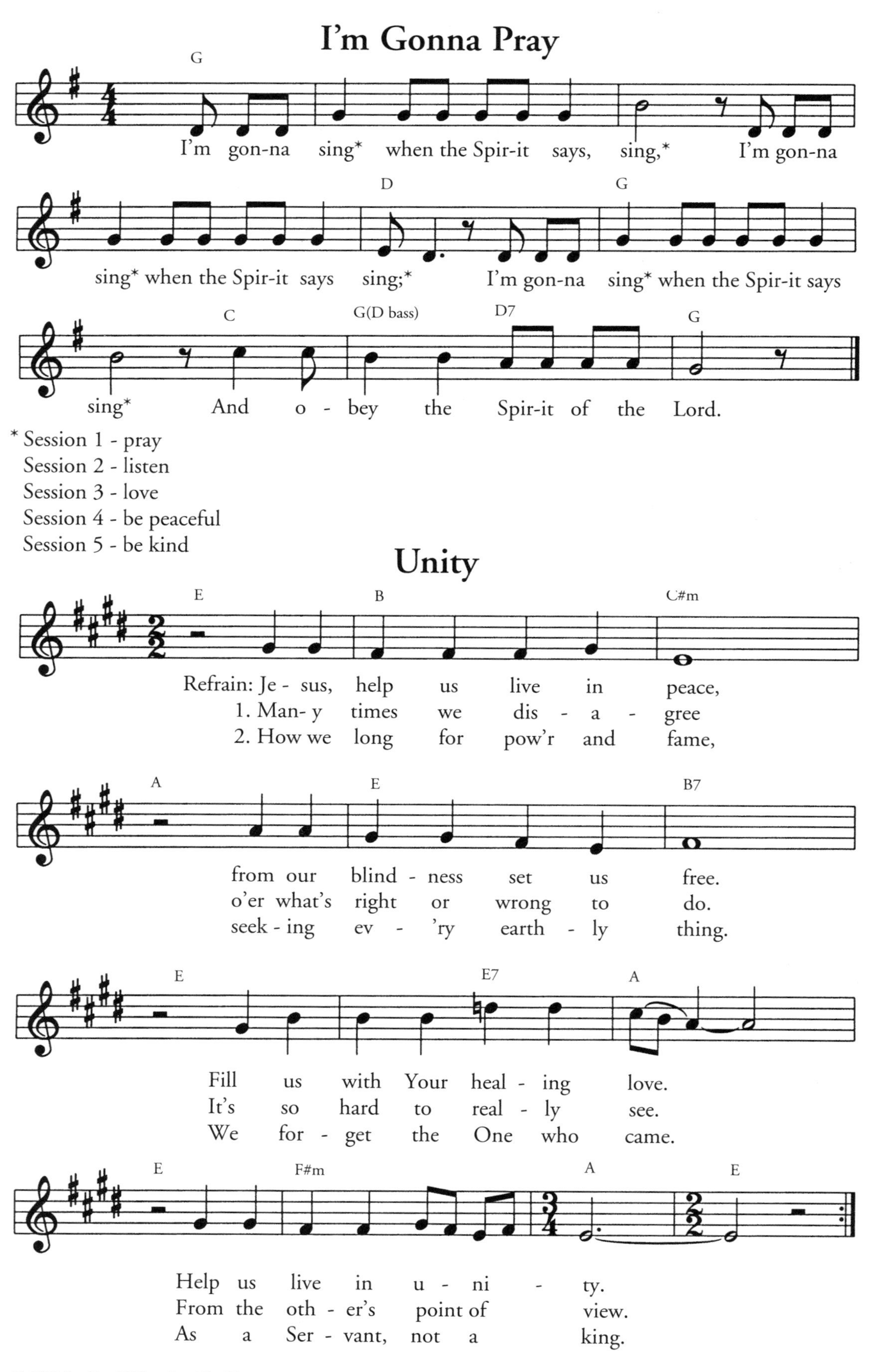

© 1971 by Gerald Derstine. Used by permission.

Make Peace

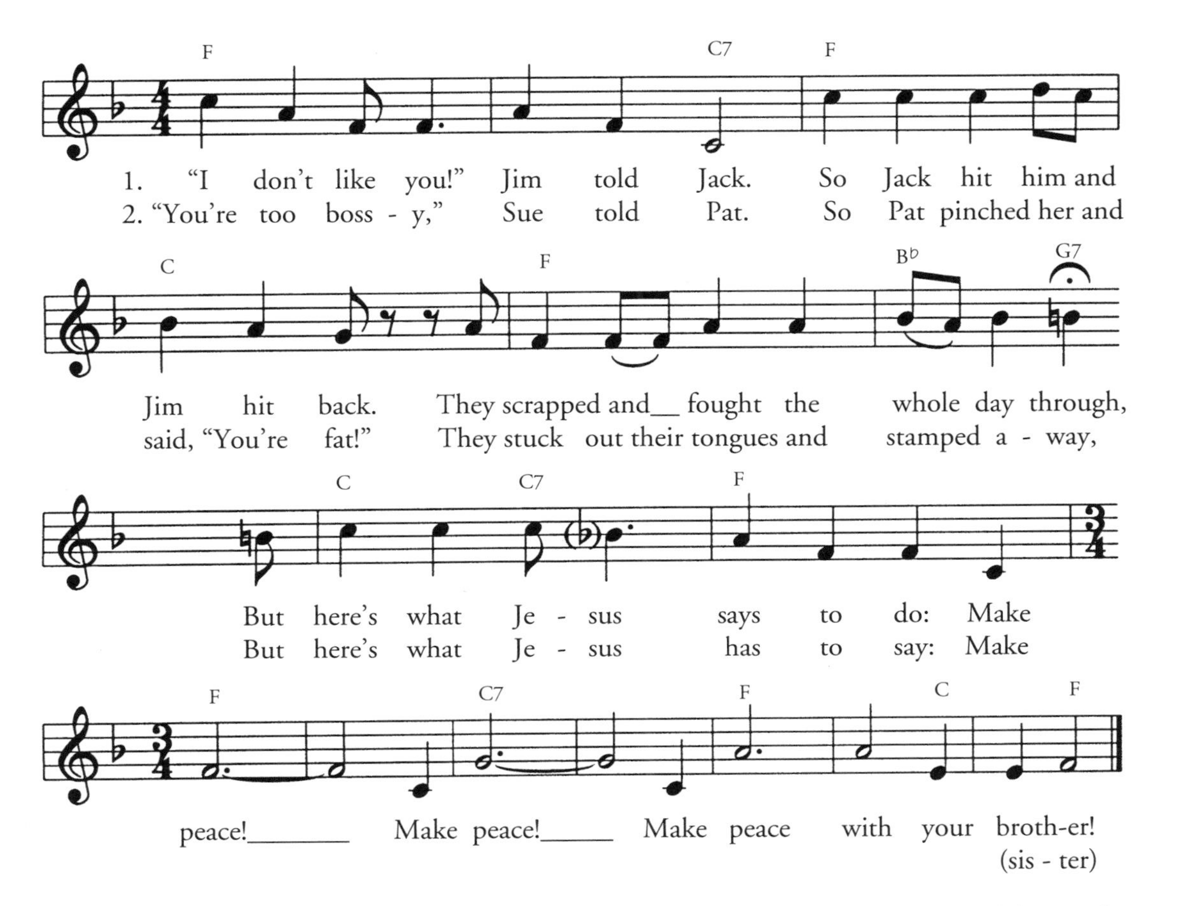

Copyright © 1974 by Herald Press, Scottdale, PA 15683. Used by permission. Reprinted from *Sing and Be Glad* © 1986 by Evangel Publishing House, Nappanee, IN 46550; Faith and Life Press, Newton, KS 67114; Mennonite Publishing House, Scottdale, PA 15683. All rights reserved.

Susan's Prayer

Words and Music by Ron Hiller and Claire Goodfellow. Copyright © 1980 Song Support, Stn. "C" Box 722, Kitchener, ON N2G 4B6. All rights reserved. Used by permission.

Optional Songs

Include other appropriate songs with which the children may be familiar. These songs fit the theme of the program but have not been reprinted:

"Love, Love, Love," by Lois Brokering (*Becoming God's Peacemakers*, Newton, Kans.: Faith & Life Press, 1992, page 133).

"I Will Hear," by Irma C. Collignon (*I Am Somebody God Loves*, Newton, Kans.: Faith & Life Press, 1993, page 116).

"Ah-la-la-la-la" (Jesus Is a Friend).

"Pass It On," Kurt Kaiser (*Sing and Be Glad,* Nappanee, Ind.: Evangel Press; Newton, Kans.: Faith & Life Press; Scottdale, Pa.: Mennonite Publishing House, 1986, p. 100).

"Magic Penny," Malvina Reynolds (*Becoming God's Peacemakers*, Newton, Kans.: Faith & Life Press, 1992, page 141).

Talk and Move Resource

Introduction

Programme

During Talk and Move the children review the Bible story and make applications to their own lives. Each session begins with an active game to help the children exercise their large muscles. The game is tied into the theme. Active learning continues as the group reviews the story through another game or creative drama followed by discussion. The discussion plays an important role. Through it the leaders discover if the children understood the theme and if learning has taken place (see Leaders and responsibilities, pages 12-17).

Leadership

The Talk and Move leader needs good communication skills, should enjoy active games, be enthusiastic and energetic, and encourage children to become active participants. The leader helps the Group leaders participate by informing them of the proposed activities and asking for their assistance, especially during discussion and debriefing times. If the group is large, find an assistant to help set up with the games and changeover times.

Preparation

Read through the entire Talk and Move Resource section to familiarize yourself with the session plans. Meet with the other resource leaders (Pray and Learn; Make and Take) to find out what is happening in their sessions.

Talk together about ways to integrate what will be said in the rotation sessions.

Before the session, collect props and materials needed for the games. Make copies of printed materials as listed.

When the children arrive, be ready to begin immediately. Follow the time guidelines closely. Pace the activities so that you have time for everything planned. If you have time at the end of your session, play some active games from an earlier session or a favourite game of the children. Encourage collaborative and cooperative games.

Session plans for Talk and Move

Session 1

Hannah

Theme: Loving God by Praying
Bible Text: 1 Samuel 1:1–2:1-11
Story Focus: Hannah's love for God was demonstrated in her prayer life. She trusted God to answer her prayer. She fulfilled her promise to God when she took Samuel to the temple to live with Eli.
Faith Focus: We show that we love God when we talk to God. We trust God to hear and answer us when we pray.

Anticipated Outcomes

1. Children will review the story of Hannah.
2. Through the active learning the children will recognize obstacles to prayer and will be encouraged to trust that God hears them when they pray.

Materials

- Items for an obstacle course: old tires, hula hoops, chairs, small benches, ropes, wood crates, etc.
- Paper or cardboard pieces
- Markers, tape
- Stopwatches (one per team)
- Outlines for the game *Hopscotch* (chalk, limestone, masking tape, rope)
- Small stones or pieces of wood for *Hopscotch* markers

Method

Bible story review

Warm-up activity: Run an *Obstacles to Prayer Course.*

1. Set up a number of short obstacle courses using items in the materials list. To make the game go quickly, have one course set up to accommodate six to eight people. Each course should have four obstacles. Give instructions for

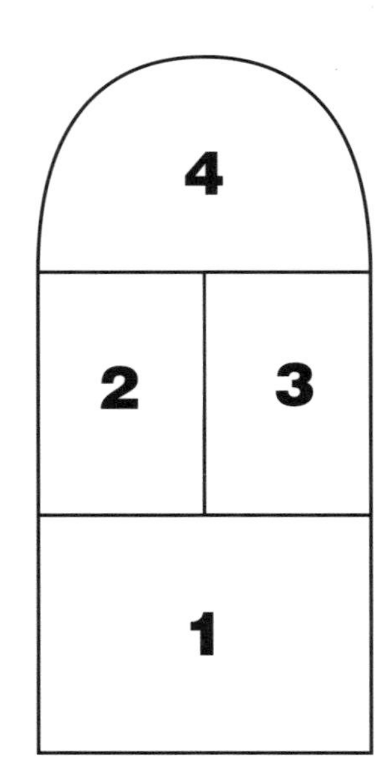

each team to run, jump, climb, and/or crawl along the course. Ask adult leaders to keep track of the time it takes the entire group to run the course.

2. When the groups have completed the course once, gather together for a brief discussion. Review the story of Hannah, using the focus of prayer and the obstacles that might have stood between her and God. What might have prevented Hannah from praying or talking to God? (sadness or anger because she had no children; teased/mocked because she had no children; repeated prayers with no answer from God; priest who did not understand).

3. Write each obstacle Hannah faced on a piece of paper or cardboard and ask a child to tape it onto one of the obstacles on the course. You may use duplicates for each obstacle course.

4. Have each group run the course again, trying to better the time of the first run. Before the run begins, ask the group to remove the obstacle that they feel was Hannah's biggest barrier.

5. Repeat the course, removing the obstacles one at a time and keeping record of the time it takes to run each course. Compare the times, noting how much easier it is to follow the course when there are no obstacles in the way.

6. Debrief in one large group. Talk about Hannah's refusal to allow obstacles to get in the way of her relationship with God.

She loved God and she trusted that God would hear her prayers. When God answered her prayer for a baby, Hannah thanked God for listening to her.

Application

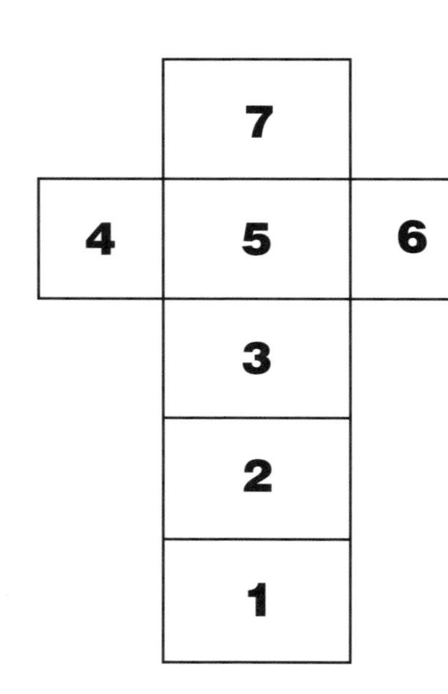

1. Talk about the things that prevent us from talking with God. Invite suggestions. Spend time in quiet reflection. Have each person think about something that may make them forget to talk with God regularly. Distribute small stones or wood pieces to represent this obstacle. Use the stone as a personal marker for the game of *Hopscotch.* The children may have to mark them in some way for personal identification.

2. Play the game *Hopscotch.* Form groups of no more than four children. Assign younger children to the simplified shape. Older children will require the more difficult cross shape. See illustrations.

Rules: The youngest child begins by throwing her or his marker onto the number one square. She hops over her marker (i.e., avoiding the obstacle to prayer), hops on the other squares to the end, turns around, and on her return, again avoids square number one. The second person does the same.

When each person has completed the first round, the first person throws her marker to the second square. She must avoid squares one and two because of the markers.

The game continues until all have reached the final square with their markers or until time is called by the leader.

Older children may play the game using the regular *Hopscotch* rules. However, encourage them to make up new rules for the game. Stress creativity and collaboration rather than competition. How can everyone be a winner?

Closing activity

Obstacle toss

Gather as a large group. Remind the children that God wants us to pray and to trust in God. God wants us to remove the obstacles that prevent us from praying.

Symbolize a willingness to let go of the obstacles to prayer by tossing away the obstacle markers used in the *Hopscotch* game. If stones have been used and there is a safe place to throw them, have the children throw them as far away as possible. Otherwise, have a bucket or basket ready for tossing them.

Have the children take one last run around the "obstacle-less" track on their way to the next activity.

Dismiss the children to their next activity.

Session 2

Samuel

Theme: Loving God by Listening
Bible Text: 1 Samuel 2:18-21, 26; 3:1-21
Story Focus: When Samuel realized that God was calling him, he responded by listening to God's voice.
Faith Focus: We show that we love God when we listen for God's voice and respond.

Anticipated Outcomes

1. Children will review the story of Samuel.
2. Children will learn to cultivate and trust their inner voice to help them make the right choices and decisions in life.

Materials

- Questions for the game show
- Props, clothing, etc., for the game show hosts
- Timer or buzzer

Method

Bible story review

Warm-up game: Play *Sammy Says.*

This game is a variation of *Simon Says.* The purpose of the game is to encourage the children to exercise their large muscles and to work on their listening skills.

The leader will tell the children to do something, but the actions will not go with the words. The children should follow what is being said, not what they see being done. They will have to listen carefully to what is being said. For example, the leader might say "Sammy says, touch your toes" at the same time she is placing her hands on her head.

In order to advance, the children must touch their toes, not their heads. As leader, give instructions that get the children moving (run on the spot, do sit-ups, do deep-knee bends, swing arms, etc.).

Temple Listen and Learn Game Show

Review the story in the form of a television game show with hosts Samuel and Eli, who invite the children to help them solve their listening problems. Samuel and Eli can play their parts with humour, wear offbeat hats or weird clothing, use mikes, props, and other materials to invite active participation of the children.

The object of the game is to help Samuel and Eli solve their "hearing problems" by having the children suggest solutions.

Directions

1. Divide the children into groups of four or five in the three age categories (K-1, 2-3, 4-5).
2. Assign a group leader to each group (or age-group). The role of the leader is to encourage but not give suggestions or solutions. Let the children be the creative problem-solvers.
3. The leader will introduce the game show hosts, Sam and Eli. (You may wish to have the children close their eyes and pretend to be in the temple at Shiloh where Sam and Eli appear and begin the show.)
4. Sam and Eli welcome the children, thanking them for coming to help them solve their "listening" problems. They talk about the fact that they did not recognize the voice of God speaking to them even though they both live in a temple. Samuel is fearful that he will not recognize God's voice again. Eli wants to assure him that God speaks in many ways, but he, too, is afraid he will not recognize the signs of God's presence. Both ask the audience to help them solve their problems by listening to the voice of God within each of them.
5. Distribute the first set of questions. See pages 68-69 for the questions for each age-group. All groups in each age division should receive the same question. Different groups may come up with different solutions. God can speak in different ways to the same issue. Encourage creative problem solving among the groups.
6. Allow a total of three minutes for discussion in the small groups. Use a timer or buzzer to signal the end of discussion. During this discussion time, each group should brainstorm creative ways to solve the problem. After the buzzer, the group must agree on the one best response to give to Sam and Eli.
7. Gather the groups together. Sam and Eli will read the questions. The groups will give their answers with fanfare, cheering, and clapping. The judge (an impartial adult, if possible) will hold up a card with a "judging" word for each answer. See the box titled Judging Words for suggestions.
8. Continue this format with the second set of questions. If the group is small, there may be time for the third set of questions. Repeat this activity two or three times, depending upon the number of groups.

Note: To make this more active, have children run to the hosts to pick up their questions, do large-muscle activity after each set of questions, jump up and down after the judging, etc. A creative host team can involve the children so that both their minds and bodies are active.

9. To end the game, Sam and Eli thank everyone for their help and then leave.

Judging Words

Great idea!

Fantastic!

I don't think so.

Try again.

Creative!

Super creative!

Awesome answer!

Application

Meet in your regular groups and have the Group leaders guide the discussion. Talk about the ways we listen to God to help us make decisions.

What guidelines do we follow for doing the right thing? How do we know when it is the right answer? Who can we trust to help us make the right decisions? God helps us to listen with our heart, to know deep down inside what is right and wrong. Other people can also help us: friends, pastors, parents, Sunday school teachers, or other trusted adults at church. Sometimes it helps to ask several other people. Then you know if you are on the right track.

Closing activity

Play *Sammy Says* again. This time the children must follow your actions. If you do not say "Sammy says," they are not to follow. Include activities that exercise their large muscles.

Dismiss the children to their next activity.

Temple Listen and Learn Game Show Questions

Kindergarten-grade 1

1. I was asleep in the temple, and I heard a voice calling me. I didn't know who it was. What things could I have done?
2. My parents have told me never to leave the temple unless Eli says it is okay. What should I do if my brothers come and want me to leave the temple and play with them? Should I go and play with them? To whom do I listen? Why?
3. My parents tell me not to cross the street unless an adult is with me. When my friends tell me it is all right to cross the street with them, what should I do? To whom do I listen? Why?

Grades 2-3

1. We are in a hurry to get to the ball field because it will soon be dark. My friends say it won't matter if we climb over the fence and go through the garden next door. What should I say or do? Why?
2. When we are playing with Jenny, some of the kids call her names and tease her about her weight. What should I say or do? Why?
3. Abdul comes from Israel. He doesn't know our language or games. When we want to play simple games, he doesn't know any of the rules. What should I do? Why?

Grades 4-5

1. My neighbour Suzannah is on the temple steps crying because her pet lamb was killed by a runaway chariot. My ball team is coming up the path now to get me for a game of field ball. They think only sissies cry. What should I say or do? Why?
2. My best friend, Daniel, told me that his stepfather hurt him at home last night. He wants to run away so he doesn't get hurt again. He also told me that he will get into big trouble if he tells anyone. Now that I know his secret, what should I do or say? Why?
3. Every day Leah and Jacob come to temple school without having had

breakfast. During lunchtime they want to trade what they have—olives and figs—for something in my lunch basket. This morning during playtime, I caught them going through the lunch baskets and taking food. What should I say or do? Why?

Session 3

Jonathan

Theme: Loving God by Loving Others
Bible Text: 1 Samuel 20:1-42
Bible Background: 1 Samuel 18 and 19
Story Focus: Jonathan risked his life for his best friend, David, though it meant danger for him.
Faith Focus: We show that we love God when we are a true friend.

Anticipated Outcome

1. The children will review the story of the friendship between Jonathan and David.
2. The children will consider how this story illustrates a loving, covenantal relationship with God.
3. The children will learn what it means to be a "true" friend.

Materials

- Ties for a three-legged race
- Ropes for marking start and finish lines
- Stopwatch
- Frisbees (plastic or made from two paper plates stapled together), one for every three children
- Course markers: hula hoops, old tires, balloon markers, arrows, or footprints, etc.
- Cards for assigning stations along the course

Method

Bible story review

Warm-up activity: Run a three-legged race.

1. As the children gather, have them find a partner who is about the same height and build. Have partners stand side by side and link arms.

2. Tie their two inside legs together for the three-legged race. Line the pairs at the starting line and point out the finishing line a short distance away.

3. Encourage the pairs to run the course. Clock how long it takes before the entire group is across the line. Repeat the race several times. Form teams and encourage each other. The race is against the clock, not against another team.

1. Debrief together in one group. Talk about how each person helped the other, how it felt to be helped, what this game may tell us about friendship.

2. Review the story of the friendship between David and Jonathan, using these "I wonder" questions:

- I wonder how David felt when Jonathan risked his life for him.
- I wonder how Jonathan felt knowing that his father hated his best friend.
- I wonder if it was hard for Jonathan to keep being David's friend when he knew it would cause problems.
- I wonder when it might be the right thing to disobey your parent for a friend. When might friendship be more important than family?
- I wonder what this story tells us about God and friendship.

Application

Play the game *Going on a Jonathan Walk.* The purpose of this game is to encourage the children to talk about right choices they must make about their friendships. The Group leader can facilitate discussion and help the children to think creatively about their responses.

1. Beforehand, set up a circular course with six or more stations. At each station have sets of questions and instructions. See page 72 for question cards. Move the group clockwise to the next station. Stations can be marked by balloons, tires, chairs, etc. Suggestions for ways to move from one station to the next are given with the answers.

2. Divide the children into two age/grade groupings (K-2, 3-5). At each station, place two sets of questions (colour-coded), one for each age-grouping (see page 72). Have an adult at each station to help the younger groups. Each group will begin at a different station.

3. The group removes the question from their colour-coded envelope, reads the situation, talks about possible solutions, and together chooses the best one. The group may check their solution against the answer given. If it is close or, better yet, a more creative solution, they follow the instructions for traveling to the next station.

4. The walk ends when each group returns to its starting station.

Debrief. Meet in one large group or in your small groups. What did the children learn about being a friend? What can they do to be a good friend?

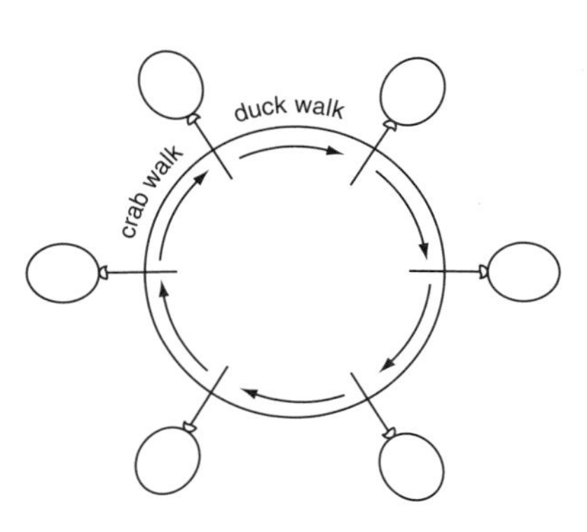

Closing activity

Take a Friendship Stand. Ask the children to find their partners from the three-legged race. Sit back-to-back on the ground and hook arms. Partners try to stand up without using their hands. When one team has successfully accomplished the task, have them find another team and try the same with four persons, then six, then eight. Close with the challenge that in order to have good friends, each person must be a good friend.

Dismiss the children to the next activity.

Going on a Jonathan Walk

Questions

Kindergarten-grade 2

Adapt the questions to suit the props you have. Cut apart the question cards for each age-group. Tape the question to an index card. Tape the answer and moving instructions to the back of the card. Place in a coloured envelope.

Read the question to the group. Read the three options and have the group agree upon the best answer. Be sure to cover up the answers while you read the questions.

STATION 1

My friend is crying by herself. The other kids say she is a crybaby and to leave her alone.

What do I do?

A. Go and sit with her.
B. Ask her if she is all right, then go and play.
C. Find out what is wrong and help her solve her problem.

Answer: C

Move to the next station doing the "crab walk" (with your body facing the sun, walk on hands and feet).

STATION 2

Maria told me I can be her best friend if I do not invite the new person, Marco, to play with us. What do I do?

A. Say, "I will be Marco's best friend instead."
B. Ask Marco over and find a game that the three of us can play together.
C. Say that there are lots of kids here, so Marco can find someone else to play with.

Answer: B

Move to the next station doing the "duck walk" (grasp your ankles with your hands and waddle along).

STATION 3

Sam, from my class at school, invited me to play after school. Five minutes later, my best friend asked me to come over to play. What do I do?

A. Call Sam and say that my mom says I can't come over.
B. Tell my best friend I can't play today, but can come over tomorrow.
C. Tell Sam I can only play for half an hour, then go to my friend's house afterwards.

Answer: B

Move to the next station by skipping with or without a skipping rope.

STATION 4

My friends are coming over to play with my new birthday toys. My mom says I must include my little sister. What do I do?

A. Give my sister one of my new toys and let her play with us.
B. Get out my sister's toys and let her play by herself beside us.
C. Play a game of hide-and-seek and my sister can be It.

Answer: A

Move to the next station by running back-to-back with a partner. Stand back-to-back, link arms, and travel as quickly as you can.

STATION 5

I want to play a game of sports outside. My friend wants to play a computer game. What do I do?

A. We talk it over and do both activities.
B. We talk it over and decide to find something we both want to do.
C. We play what my friend wants to play.

Answer: B

Move to the next station by running as fast as you can all around the outside of the course in the opposite direction (counterclockwise).

STATION 6

I am not allowed to invite my friends into our backyard unless I ask my parents first. One day I heard my friend yelling and saw him being chased down the street by a bully. What should I do?

A. Tell him to come into the backyard where it is safe.
B. Run and ask my mom if he can come into the backyard.
C. Tell him to run home.

Answer: A

Do ten sit-ups and wait for your group leader.

Questions for the Jonathan Walk (Grades 3-5)

Read the question to the group. Read the three options and have the group agree upon the best answer.

STATION 1

My friend, Sara, has cancer. Her treatment caused her hair to fall out. She is sitting alone, feeling sad. The other kids don't want to include her in any activity. What do I do?

1. Say that there are other kids like her to play with.
2. Say that I won't play with my friends unless they include Sara.
3. Talk with my friends, explaining that she is the same as we are and can play with us.

Answer: 3

Move to the next station with everyone joining hands and running backwards.

STATION 2

Maria told me I can be her best friend if I do not invite the new person, Marco, to play with us. What do I do?

1. Say Maria will still be my friend but not my best friend, and go and play with Marco.
2. Find something the three of you can do together.
3. Introduce Marco to another person and tell them to be best friends.

Answer: 2

Move to the next station by running twice, counterclockwise, around the entire course.

STATION 3

My best friend phoned me to come over after school. Five minutes later, Sam, the most popular kid in my class at school, called up and invited me to his/her home. What do I do?

1. Call my best friend and say that my mom says I can't come over.
2. Tell Sam I can't come over today, but tomorrow would be fine.
3. Tell my friend that I can only play for half an hour, then go to Sam's house for the rest of the time.

Answer: 2

Move to the next station by doing the duck walk (grasp your ankles with your hands).

STATION 4

At school my friends and I arranged to go to the park to play ball. When I got home, my mom reminded me that I had promised to play with my little brother. What do I do?

1. I take him with me, along with some of his toys for him to play with by himself.
2. We let him play with us; he chases after the ball when it gets away from us.
3. We let him play with us, and make the rules easier for him.

Answer: 3

Move to the next station by repeating a hop, step, and jump.

STATION 5

I want to watch a video. My friend wants to play computer games. What do I do?

1. I give in to my friend and play computer games.
2. We talk it over and decide to do both activities.
3. We find something else that we both like to do.

Answer: 3

Move to the next station by turning somersaults or crawling.

STATION 6

My parents do not come home until 6 o'clock. I am not allowed to open the door to anyone unless one parent is home. My friend and her brother saw a strange man climb over their backyard fence. They ran to my place because they were home alone and they were afraid. What do I do?

1. Let my friend and her brother into my house. Explain to my parents when they get home.
2. Let my friend and her brother into my house but make them promise not to tell my parents.
3. Don't open the door.

Answer: 1

Do 20 sit-ups with a partner and wait for your group leader.

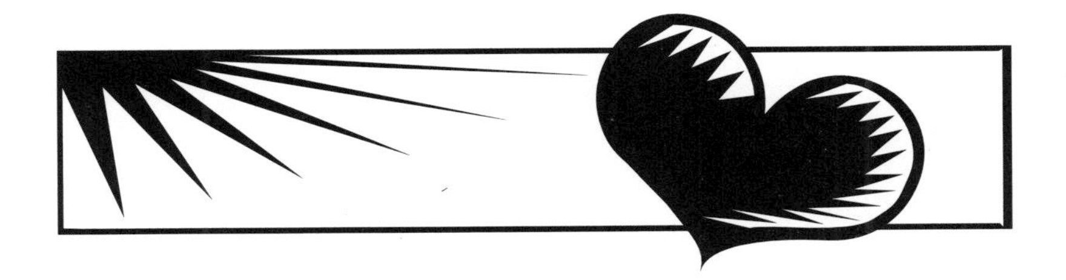

Session 4

Abigail

Theme: Loving God by Making Peace
Bible Text: 1 Samuel 25:1-38
Story Focus: Abigail demonstrated creative thinking skills in order to keep peace between two enemies, Nabal and David.
Faith Focus: We show that we love God when we solve our problems in peaceful ways.

Anticipated Outcomes

1. The children will review the story of Abigail.
2. The children will have the opportunity to think creatively in resolving everyday conflicts.

Materials

- Balls of all shapes and sizes, Frisbees, and/or hoops, balloons blown up and tied inside a plastic bag
- A tape recorder
- Music appropriate for exercising

Method

Bible story review

Warm-up activity: Do a Shake Your Bod! activity.

1. Allow each child to choose a ball or another piece of sports equipment. Tell them to move to the music, exercising their arms, torso, legs, and entire body. Encourage them to find creative ways to use the piece of equipment in their exercise without moving off the spot. After a few moments, have them find a partner and do some movements together. One will start with a simple routine. The other will mimic the first and add to it. Add another person to the group and begin a new routine. Continue until groups of five children

have formed.

2. Look for alternative ways to solve a problem. Try this activity or make up one using your own set of rules.

Play an active game using these rules.

Rules:

- Everyone participates.
- Everyone has to move some body part.
- Everyone cooperates rather than competes.

Supplies:

Balls or balloons in a bag

Solve one of these dilemmas using the three rules.

- Pass a ball or balloon around the circle without using any hands.
- Pass a bag of balloons around the circle using only your feet.

Have fun and then talk about the process. How did the group work to follow the three rules? What did you learn about working together?

3. "Abigail's Dilemma" (page 77)

Read "Abigail's Dilemma" to the groups. Ask the children to think and talk about the different ways that this story could have ended peacefully. Encourage creative problem solving. Have the group choose their most creative, yet realistic, solution to Abigail's dilemma, and be prepared to share with the other groups.

Application

1. Discuss modern dilemmas. Remind the children that we live with conflict all the time. It is part of life. What is important, though, is how we deal with conflict when it happens. God wants us to be peacemakers, to find ways to resolve conflict without fighting, putting someone down, ignoring them, or hurting them in any way. How can we learn to be better problem-solvers? Brainstorm options: imagine the problem being solved, plan ahead, pray for guidance, keep communication open and honest.

2. Distribute the two Dilemma Cards (page 77) to each group (the same five people in groups) and ask them to choose one of the situations to solve in skit form. Follow the same format as above: brainstorm ways to resolve the conflict, choose the best way, and be prepared to act it out for the group. Allow time for discussion and preparation. The group may choose a dilemma of their own.

Note: For Jordan's Dilemma, #2, assign the role of the thirteen-year-olds to the younger two children.

3. Invite the groups to present their skits. To save time, you may wish to have all of the groups who prepared for Dilemma #1 present it to each other. Do the same for the Dilemma #2 and Dilemma #3 groups.

Debrief. What did you learn about being a peacemaker? How does listening to our inner voice (God's Spirit) help us to be more creative problem-solvers?

Closing activity

Peacemakers' cheer

Create a cheer with arm movements and shouts.

Give me a P (response) P
Give me an E (response) E
etc....
What do ya say? (response) PEACEMAKER
Say it louder! (response) PEACEMAKER!!
Say it again! (response) PEACEMAKER!!!
YEAH, GOD! (response) YEAH, GOD!
End with a "high five" to the person beside you.

Dismiss the children to the next activity.

Dilemma Cards

#1
Abigail's Dilemma
Nabal has just discovered that David and his soldiers want to join the feast he is preparing. Being selfish and miserly, Nabal does not want to share his food with outsiders. When David heard this, he became very angry because he was hungry and because he had protected Nabal's property from thieves and wild animals. Both men are very angry and decide to fight it out in the field. They are standing face-to-face when Abigail finds out about the conflict. As she rushes out to the field, she is desperately thinking of what she can do to stop this fight that will surely mean someone's death. What do you think she should say? What should she do? What solution can she offer that will make the men stop their fighting? How can she be a peacemaker?

#2
Jordan's Dilemma
Chris and Terry are thirteen-year-old friends. They are always at the park on weekends. There they do not allow anyone else to play on the equipment. Keri and Robin, seven-year-old friends, are only allowed to go to the park on Saturday afternoons. Today is Saturday. The three older friends will not let the younger children near the play equipment. Keri and Robin start to complain about this bullying, and the other three would really like to start a fight with them. Jordan, who is ten years old, hears the commotion and comes to see what is going on. How can this dilemma be solved peacefully?

Note: For Jordan's Dilemma, #2, assign the role of the thirteen-year-olds to the two younger children.

#3

Marta's Dilemma

In vacation Bible school, children your ages are asked to draw pictures of Jesus and some of his disciples or followers for a mural. Esau, who comes from Somalia, draws a picture of Jesus; Maria, from Honduras, draws Martha; John, from Canada, draws Peter; and Jane, also from Canada, draws John. When the pictures are completed and glued onto the mural, John and Jane are upset because the pictures of Jesus and Martha showed them with dark-brown skin colour. They said that all the pictures they ever saw showed Jesus with the same colour skin as theirs. They told Esau and Maria to draw the pictures over again "the right way." Marta, a visitor from Palestine, is asked to solve the dilemma, since she lived close to where Jesus had lived a long time ago. How can this dilemma be solved peacefully?

Session 5

David

Theme: Loving God by Showing Kindness
Bible Text: 2 Samuel 4:4; 9:1-13
Story Focus: David showed kindness and brought Mephibosheth into his home.
Faith Focus: We show that we love God when we are kind, just, and generous.

Anticipated Outcomes

1. Children will review the story of David's act of loving-kindness.
2. Children will learn that as they listen for God's voice, they will find ways to show loving-kindness.
3. Children will learn that acts of kindness are acts of justice done from a motive of love for God.

Materials

- Narrow boards, one for each team of five
- Rope or cloths to restrict walking of each Mephibosheth
- Snack foods in a wicker basket (chocolates, fruit, cookies)

Method

Bible story review

1. Do a warm-up activity: Play *Frozen Touch Tag.*

Choose the oldest or tallest person to be It. If there is a large group, have two Its. Play the usual game of tag. When a person is tagged by It, she or he must stop, place one hand over the part of the body that was tagged, and freeze. To be freed, this person must be touched by someone who has not been tagged. However, the "freed" person must run with her or his hand covering the part that was originally tagged.

Debrief. Talk about feelings experienced during the game. How did it feel to be frozen? How did it feel to have a "disability" after you were freed? How did it feel to be It? What did you like or dislike about the rules to this game? Would Mephibosheth have enjoyed this game? Why or why not?

2. Play *The Feast of David* game. Number off in groups of five. The oldest will be Mephibosheth. Other children will be David, Abigail, Zodiac, and Ziba. Ahead of time, set up the "stage" for the game. Mark off an area with ropes to represent the ditch. Abigail is on one side (palace side) holding a treat for the others on her team. Across the ditch is a narrow piece of wood. Set the planks at a distance of about three meters, three yards, from each other so there is room for each group to move (see illustration).

Introduction: David and Abigail live in the king's palace. Around the palace is a ditch filled with quicksand. The bridge that people normally use to get into the palace was wrecked in a freak windstorm. A narrow plank of wood is the only way to get across this ditch. One's life is in danger if one steps off the plank. Abigail is on the palace side ready to host a great feast in honour of Mephibosheth's arrival. David and Mephibosheth and the two servants are on the other side of the ditch and are very anxious to get to the feast.

Conditions:

1. Each child plays the role of the character as assigned.

2. If someone steps off the plank, the group must all return to the other side, except for Abigail.

3. Being a polite hostess, Abigail will not serve the feast until her entire group is assembled on the palace side of the ditch.

4. Mephibosheth has his legs tied together at the ankle so he cannot walk by himself.

Play the game.

Debrief. Sit together for discussion. Ask the children to tell how they felt playing the role of the character to which they were assigned. How did Mephibosheth feel? How did you feel about Mephibosheth? What were the creative ways used to get across the ditch? Did anyone think about putting the planks together and working together with another group?

Application

1. Talk about the kind of justice David showed. He looked after his friend's son because it was the right thing to do. He showed kindness to Mephibosheth because it was the right thing to do. God expects us to "love kindness" and do acts of kindness because it is the right thing to do, because it is a way to show that we love God. Acts of loving-kindness are not always easy. To show kindness means to show respect for another, to treat the other the way you wish to be treated, the way God would treat you or another person, to consider each person to be of equal value.

2. When we play competitive games, it is sometimes difficult to treat everyone equally and with the same respect. Often our desire to win becomes more important than our treatment of other people. What rules for "loving-kindness" would be acceptable in a normally competitive game?

3. Choose an active game that can have the rules changed quite simply. Soccer is a good choice. Decide first how the teams could be determined in a fair way. Next, determine the rules so that each person is given equal value and respect, regardless of ability. Some suggestions are: three different people must touch the ball before a goal can be scored; the ball must alternate between boys and girls (i.e., a boy must pass the ball to a girl); extra points are scored for passing the ball; everyone plays in "crab walk" style; everyone over age ten hops on one foot, etc. Review the rules in light of David's justice: would he feel that the rules indicate loving-kindness?

4. Play the game for a few minutes. Then stop and ask if everyone is feeling included and valued in the game or if there needs to be some revision to the rules. Continue to play the game.

Debrief. How did you like the game? What did you learn about yourself and your feelings of competition? How did it feel to have a disability? How did you act toward people who had a disability? What did you learn about "loving-kindness" through this game?

Variations: To emphasize inclusion of everyone, distribute "visible disabilities" during the game (someone is blindfolded, someone sits on a chair, someone wears earmuffs, someone wears large boots or a helmet). If possible, have everyone experience a disability at some point during the game. Another variation is to have all the children find a different way to move: crawling, hopping, jumping. No running is allowed.

Dismiss the children to the next activity.

Pray and Learn Resource

Introduction

Programme

During Pray and Learn the children learn the memory text, talk about their relationship with God, experience prayer, and have their snack.

Ideas are given for fun ways to learn the memory verses, both for the overall *Loving God* theme and for each session. Each session begins with a review of the theme memory verses and the introduction of the daily verse. Spend about five to seven minutes on memory learning each session.

For a complete listing of the Bible memory passages in both the New Revised Standard Version and the New International Version, see pages 105-108. You may choose between these versions or use another version. Ideas and ways to memorize the Scriptures are found on pages 105-109.

Each session includes discussion about prayer, a prayer time, and making a prayer bracelet. Prayer time may be a new experience for many of the children. Start with only a few moments of silent prayer. Each day you may wish to add more time. Be sensitive to the time the children are able to spend alone. If the children cannot pray alone and silently, meet in small groups with an adult leader for prayer time.

Use the song "Lord, Listen to Your Children" (page 57) to introduce the prayer time each session. Teach it during the first session or use a tape recording. The music can help to calm the children and bring them into the presence of God.

The snack is served during this time. When it is not written into the session as a part of the prayer time, you may wish to offer it at the end of the session for the first group and at the beginning of the session for the second and third groups.

Leadership

The Pray and Learn leader should have good communication skills to lead discussion, enjoy memory games and activities, feel comfortable in praying audibly, and talk about God from a personal perspective. Children can sense if the leader is uncomfortable. It is vital that she or he has a growing personal relationship with God and is willing to talk about that with the children. If the group is large, it would be good to have assistants who will meet with smaller groups for prayer and discussion. See Leaders and responsibilities, page 12, for more ideas.

Preparation

Read through the entire Pray and Learn Resource section so that you have a complete understanding of this part of the programme. Prepare the memory verse materials ahead of time and have them ready when the children arrive.

Have ready the lengths of coloured embroidery threads: blue, yellow, red, white, and green. These colours match with the colours being used for the door-hanging panels each session (see page 113). Prepare additional materials that are unique to each session.

Consult with the Snack coordinator about the snacks. Be sure that the snacks are ready for each group when requested.

Reinforcement of the theme

Take time to relate the activities to the Bible story and to the overall theme of *Loving God*. The prayer and reflection times offer the children the opportunity to express their love for God through prayers, artwork, discussion, and song.

Session plans for Pray and Learn

Session 1

Hannah

Theme: Loving God by Praying
Bible Text: 1 Samuel 1:1—2:1-11
Story Focus: Hannah's love for God was demonstrated in her prayer life. She trusted that God would answer her prayer. She lived out her love for God when she fulfilled her promise and took Samuel to the temple to live with Eli.
Faith Focus: We show that we love God when we talk to God. We trust that God will hear and answer us when we pray.

Bible Memory Texts

"You shall love the Lord your God with all your heart, and with all your soul, and with all your strength, and with all your mind; and your neighbor as yourself" (Luke 10:27, NRSV).

"'Love the Lord your God with all your heart and with all your soul and with all your strength and with all your mind'; and, 'Love your neighbor as yourself'" (Luke 10:27, NIV).

And what does the Lord require of you but to do justice, and to love kindness, and to walk humbly with your God? (Micah 6:8b, NRSV).

And what does the Lord require of you? To act justly and to love mercy and to walk humbly with your God (Micah 6:8b, NIV).

Anticipated Outcomes

1. The children will begin to learn the two memory texts.
2. The children will discover and review the different types of prayers.
3. The children will experience a time of prayer to help them understand that God hears us when we pray.

Setting

Meet in the sanctuary. Hannah went to the temple to talk with God. One of the places where we can meet God is in the church building.

Materials

- Tape recorder with quiet music or piano or guitar for live music
- Song "Lord Listen to Your Children Praying" (page 57)
- Copy of "Hannah's Prayer" (page 88)
- Snack: pretzels (not sticks)
- Pieces of blue embroidery thread, 20 to 25 cm., (8 to 10 in.), one per child (adjust size for smaller wrists)

Method

As children assemble, sing a praise song or psalm. If you are not comfortable with leading songs, play a recording of some praise songs.

Bible Memory

Introduce the two key memory texts, using several of the options suggested (see pages 105-106).

Prayer Theme

1. Say "Hannah's Prayer" together. Print it onto an overhead transparency or chart paper. Repeat the refrain together to help the younger children who may not read well. Then read the prayer together.

2. Sing songs of praise. Divide the children into groups of five or six. Assign each group a nursery rhyme tune or another familiar tune. Ask them to write a song of praise and thanks to God. Possible tune suggestions: "Mary Had a Little Lamb," "Three Blind Mice," "Frere Jacques," refrain from "Jesus Loves Me," "This Is the Day."

For example: (Tune: "Twinkle, Twinkle, Little Star")

Thank-you, thank-you, thank-you, God.
Oh, how wonderful you are!
You have made the earth, the sky.
You sent us your precious son.
Thank-you, thank-you, thank-you, God.
Oh how wonderful you are!

Allow time to prepare and present the songs.

Reflection and Prayer

1. Sing "Lord, Listen to Your Children Praying." Talk about the ways in which we can talk to God. Remind the children that we talked to God when we sang, when we read Hannah's song of praise, and when we sang the songs of praise that we wrote. We think about God when we learn the Bible verses that tell us how God wants us to live. We can talk to God in our thoughts. This is called prayer.

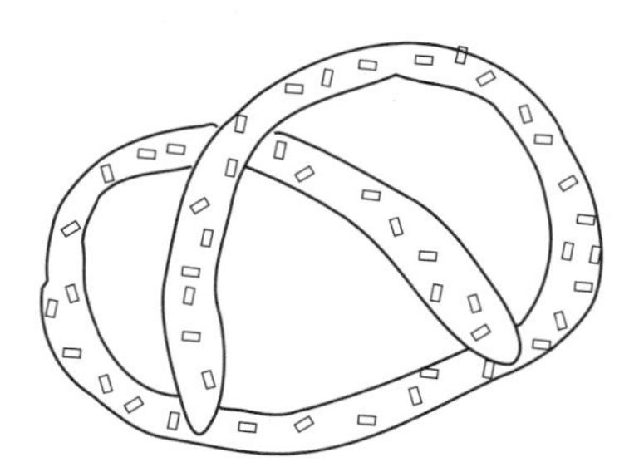

2. Share a snack. Pass a basket with pretzels, inviting each person to take one or more. Tell the pretzel story: "The pretzel is made in the shape of crossed arms. When pretzels were first made, they were called little arms. It is believed that pretzels were first made by monks in Europe. Monks spent a long time praying each day. When they prayed, they would cross their arms over their chests as a sign of reverence.

To help the children understand that praying every day was important, the monks gave the children a small reward for saying their prayers. The reward was a piece of bread dough shaped like the crossed arms of a child praying. So, as you eat your pretzel, say a silent thank-you prayer to God for listening to our prayers.

3. Hand out pieces of blue embroidery thread and have the children help each other tie the thread to each person's wrist. Explain that each day the children will receive a different coloured thread as their reminder to pray. Today's thread is blue as a reminder that God is holy and awesome, and God is our protector. We can be joyful, like Hannah, because God listens to us when we pray, both in God's house and when we are at home.

4. Invite the children to find a place in the sanctuary where they can be by themselves to pray. Ask them to sit quietly and talk to God. They may wish to thank God for something special in their lives or talk about anything they want. God has promised to listen to them and to be their friend. Encourage them to whisper their prayers to God as though God were there right beside them. Tell them to sit quietly until the music has stopped. During this silent prayer time, play the song sung earlier, or play another appropriate piece on the piano or tape recorder.

5. End this time with a closing audible prayer: "God of Hannah and the children here, thank-you for listening to our prayers. Help us to remember to say a prayer of thanks to you today whenever we look at our blue-thread bracelet. Thank-you for being an awesome God. Amen."

Dismiss the children to the next activity.

Hannah's Prayer

All: The Lord has filled my heart with joy [*Clap, clap in front.*]
I am happy because God has helped me. [*Clap, clap above head.*]
One: There is no one as holy as the Lord,
God protects us and makes us strong.
All: The Lord has filled my heart with joy [*Clap, clap.*]
I am happy because God has helped me. [*Clap, clap.*]
One: The Lord our God knows us,
and judges all that we do.
All: The Lord has filled my heart with joy. [*Clap, clap.*]
I am happy because God has helped me. [*Clap, clap.*]
One: Amen.
All: Amen.

Session 2

Samuel

Theme: Loving God by Listening
Bible Text: 1 Samuel 2:18-21, 26; 3:1-21
Story Focus: When Samuel realized that God was calling to him, he responded by listening to God's voice.
Faith Focus: We show that we love God when we listen for God's voice and respond by living out God's love.

Bible Memory Texts

"You shall love the Lord your God with all your heart, and with all your soul, and with all your strength, and with all your mind; and your neighbor as yourself" (Luke 10:27, NRSV).

"'Love the Lord your God with all your heart and with all your soul and with all your strength and with all your mind'; and, 'Love your neighbor as yourself'" (Luke 10:27, NIV).

And what does the Lord require of you but to do justice, and to love kindness, and to walk humbly with your God? (Micah 6:8b, NRSV).

And what does the Lord require of you? To act justly and to love mercy and to walk humbly with your God (Micah 6:8b, NIV).

"'Speak, Lord, for your servant is listening'" (1 Samuel 3:9b, NIV and NRSV).

Anticipated Outcomes

1. The children will review the two theme memory texts and learn the third.
2. The children will know that God speaks to them in a variety of ways.

Setting

If possible, meet out-of-doors, or in an area where the children can sit comfortably.

Materials

- Carpet, mats, or cushions
- Cassette with about ten prerecorded sounds from around home (water running, door closing, engine starting, eating, etc.)
- Paper and pencils
- Several tape recorders for taping sounds
- Pieces of yellow embroidery threads, 20 to 26 cm., (8 to 10 in.), one per child
- Crunchy snack (crackers, veggies, etc.)
- Copy of litany "Speak, Lord" (p. 91) on overhead or chart paper

Method

Bible Memory

As the children gather, involve them in memory verse review of the theme texts, using one or more of the suggestions given.

Prayer Theme

Samuel heard God's voice calling his name. When he finally recognized that it was God's voice, Samuel asked God to speak again, because he was ready to listen.

1. Think about and discuss the following questions:

- Does God speak to us today?
- How do we listen for God?
- What would help us be better listeners so we can hear God speak?

2. Try a listening activity. Divide the children into three smaller groups. Give out the following assignments:

Group A: Gather around the tape recorder. See if the group can identify all the prerecorded sounds. Talk about the importance of listening carefully to these sounds in order to identify them.

Group B: Go for a tour around the premises with a tape recorder or two. Record the sounds you hear. Prepare a list of the recorded sounds. Then make a list of nature and other sounds that can remind us of how God speaks to us.

Group C: Mime ways to communicate without sound (hugs, facial expressions, sign language, etc.). Talk about the ways we can listen and understand without words.

Reassemble. Have the groups report and present what they learned. Group A can identify the sounds. Group B can play the tape and give the others the opportunity to guess the sounds. Group C can mime their stances and have the others guess what is being communicated.

Reflection and Prayer

1. Sing "Lord, Listen to Your Children Praying."

2. Distribute the yellow embroidery threads. Explain that yellow was chosen to represent careful listening and inspiration. When we listen with all our attention, our inner self, God can speak to us and give us new thoughts. Have the children help each other tie the yellow thread next to the blue thread.

Note: If this is the first day for a child, give them a piece of blue thread as well as the yellow. Briefly explain or have the children explain what type of prayer it represents.

3. Invite the children to find a comfortable spot by themselves, but within

hearing distance of you. Guide them through the following prayer experience.

- Relax and get comfortable in your space.
- Imagine that you are in a favourite spot where you can think quietly. It may be outside or inside. Make yourself comfortable and pretend you are in that favourite spot.
- Listen to the sounds around you in your imaginary place. What do you hear that is relaxing and comforting?
- Imagine that God is beside you in your favourite spot. Welcome God to sit beside you. Tell God that you are ready to listen to what God wants to tell you. Sit quietly and wait. What might God say to you about you or your family or your friends?
  [*Allow for about thirty seconds of silence, then say:*]
- Say thank-you to God for being with you and speaking to you.
- Open your eyes and sit quietly until everyone else has opened their eyes.

4. Distribute a "crunchy" snack. During snack time, invite the children to meet again for discussion in the small groups as for the listening activity. Invite them to express how it felt for them to listen for God in this way. What did they learn about listening to God? Was it difficult to imagine a conversation with God? Encourage the children to try this prayer activity at home in a quiet place and to practice listening for and recognizing God's voice. We can imagine that God is with us any time and any place. God is everywhere. What an awesome God!

5. Close with the litany prayer of thanksgiving, "Speak, Lord." The Session 2 memory text appears in the refrain.

Dismiss the children to the next activity.

Speak, Lord

Leader: Lord, forgive us, for we are often too busy to hear you speak. Quiet our minds so that we can be open to your words.
All: Speak, Lord, for your servant is listening.
Leader: Lord, you sometimes come to us in surprising ways. We know that you can speak to us in many different ways.
All: Speak, Lord, for your servant is listening.
Leader: Lord, we want to hear you calling our names. You have chosen us before we even knew you.
All: Speak, Lord, for your servant is listening.
Leader: Lord, help us to respond in faith to your calling like Samuel did.
All: Speak, Lord, for your servant is listening.

Permission is granted to purchasers of this curriculum to photocopy this page for use with the Loving God *curriculum.*

Session 3

Jonathan

Theme: Loving God by Loving Others
Bible Text: 1 Samuel 20:1-42
Bible Background: 1 Samuel 18 and 19
Story Focus: Jonathan risked his life for his best friend, David, although it meant danger for him.
Faith Focus: We live out God's love when we are a true friend.

Bible Memory Texts

"You shall love the Lord your God with all your heart, and with all your soul, and with all your strength, and with all your mind; and your neighbor as yourself" (Luke 10:27, NRSV).

"'Love the Lord your God with all your heart and with all your soul and with all your strength and with all your mind'; and, 'Love your neighbor as yourself'" (Luke 10:27, NIV).

And what does the Lord require of you but to do justice, and to love kindness, and to walk humbly with your God? (Micah 6:8b, NRSV).

And what does the Lord require of you? To act justly and to love mercy and to walk humbly with your God (Micah 6:8b, NIV).

"'Speak, Lord, for your servant is listening'" (1 Samuel 3:9b, NIV and NRSV).

Beloved, since God loved us so much, we also ought to love one another (1 John 4:11, NRSV).

Dear friends, since God so loved us, we also ought to love one another (1 John 4:11, NIV).

Anticipated Outcomes

1. The children will review the theme texts and learn today's memory text.
2. The children will learn about God's willingness to be their friend.

Setting

Meet indoors. Have tables available for response time.

Materials

- The 1 John memory text written on puzzle pieces, enough puzzles so that each person has one piece (Puzzles can be different colours or sizes so that children can group themselves and then put their puzzle together.)
- Heart-shaped cookies for snack
- Pieces of red embroidery thread, 20 to 26 cm., 8 to 10 in., one per person
- "Letters to God" booklets (pages 95-98), enough for one per child, pages stapled or sewn together in the centre
- Pencils, pens, erasers

Method

Bible Memory

As the children gather, distribute pieces of today's memory text that has been prepared as a puzzle. Have prepared a variety of puzzles (see Materials). When a puzzle is completed, have the children shout out the verse. Gather up the puzzle pieces and redistribute. See how quickly the children can piece the puzzles the second time.

Review the other theme texts quickly, using one of the options (see pages 105-107).

Prayer Theme

The Bible story illustrates a special, true friendship between two people. This friendship symbolizes the friendship that God seeks with us.

1. Invite responses to these questions:

- How did Jonathan prove to be a good friend?
- What is needed for a true friendship? (loyalty, trust, love, risk)
- How is God a friend to us like Jonathan was to David?

2. Distribute the snack. As the children eat, encourage them to talk about their friends—what is special about them, how they demonstrate their friendship, why friends are important, etc.

Reflection and Prayer

1. Sing "Lord, Listen to Your Children Praying" as the introduction to prayer time.

2. Distribute the red embroidery threads. Have the children help each other to tie the threads beside the other two colours. Explain that the colour red was chosen because of its association with love. God loves us. The red thread will be a reminder of the love God has for us and that we, in turn, offer to God.

3. Encourage the children to offer a prayer of thanks for God's love whenever they look at their thread.

4. Give each child a "Letters to God" booklet to write or draw personal messages to God. Encourage the children to write one entry on a page of their choice during this session.

You may wish to invite someone who regularly uses a prayer journal to tell of her or his experiences in journal writing.

Close with an audible prayer. Invite the children to join hands or link arms and repeat this prayer:

Dear God, thank-you for offering to be my friend. Help me to be a friend to you. Help me to be a friend to others, too. Thank-you for loving me. I love you, too, and want to show your love by the way I live. Amen.

Dismiss the children to the next activity.

These pieces of coloured embroidery threads remind me to pray:
Blue *reminds me to be thankful to God.*
Yellow *reminds me to listen to God.*
Red *reminds me to talk to my friend, God.*
White *reminds me to ask God to help me be a peacemaker.*
Green *reminds me to ask God to show me how to be loving.*

My Letters to God

by

Memory Texts

"You shall love the Lord your God with all your heart, and with all your soul, and with all your strength, and with all your mind; and your neighbor as yourself." Luke 10:27

"What does the Lord require of you but to do justice, and to love kindness, and to walk humbly with your God?" Micah 6:8b

"Speak, Lord, for your servant is listening." 1 Samuel 3:9b

"Beloved, since God loved us so much, we also ought to love one another." 1 John 4:11

"Depart from evil, and do good; seek peace, and pursue it." Psalm 34:14

"Do good, be rich in good works, generous, and ready to share." 1 Timothy 6:18 (adapted)

Dear God ______________________________

Dear God
Dear God

Dear God.
Dear God.

Session 4

Abigail

Theme: Loving God by Making Peace
Bible Text: 1 Samuel 25:1-38
Story Focus: Abigail demonstrated creative thinking skills in order to keep peace between two enemies, Nabal and David.
Faith Focus: We live God's love when we solve our problems in peaceful ways.

Memory Texts

"You shall love the Lord your God with all your heart, and with all your soul, and with all your strength, and with all your mind; and your neighbor as yourself" (Luke 10:27, NRSV).

"'Love the Lord your God with all your heart and with all your soul and with all your strength and with all your mind'; and, 'Love your neighbor as yourself'" (Luke 10:27, NIV).

And what does the Lord require of you but to do justice, and to love kindness, and to walk humbly with your God? (Micah 6:8b, NRSV).

And what does the Lord require of you? To act justly and to love mercy and to walk humbly with your God (Micah 6:8b, NIV).

"'Speak, Lord, for your servant is listening'" (1 Samuel 3:9b, NIV and NRSV).

Beloved, since God loved us so much, we also ought to love one another (1 John 4:11, NRSV).

Dear friends, since God so loved us, we also ought to love one another (1 John 4:11, NIV).

Depart from evil, and do good; seek peace, and pursue it (Psalm 34:14, NRSV).

Turn from evil and do good; seek peace and pursue it (Psalm 34:14, NIV).

Anticipated Outcomes

1. The children will review the theme memory texts and learn the new Psalms text.

2. The children will learn that God wants them to seek peaceful solutions to conflict situations.

Setting

Meet outdoors, if possible.

Materials

- Snack of mini rice cakes or large crackers (four per child)
- Pieces of white embroidery thread, 20 to 26 cm., 8 to 10 in., one per person
- Materials for a mural: poster paint, baking pans, white cloth or newsprint, markers, soapy water, and towels

Method

Bible Memory

As children gather, have them review all the memory texts from the previous sessions. See pages 105-109 for memorizing ideas.

Teach the Psalms text, using the rhythmic ostinato method (see page 107).

Prayer Theme

Today's theme is about conflict resolution. The story of Abigail illustrates the concept that God's heroes and heroines are peacemakers. God helped Abigail come up with her creative idea that led to a peaceful solution. Abigail was able to live out God's way of peace.

1. Do a circle game activity. Have the children form a large circle as they stand and hold hands. The leader will read the statements (see page 101) and instruct the group to respond after each statement. The children should repeat the bold print after the leader says it.

Reflection and Prayer

1. Sing "Lord, Listen to Your Children Praying" as the introduction to personal prayer.

2. Distribute four small rice cakes or crackers to each person. Explain that these rice cakes or crackers represent peace. When we eat them, we can think about taking God's peace and forgiveness into our lives. Talk about the meaning of confession as a type of prayer. Sometimes we forget to live God's love. We need to ask God's forgiveness, or say we are sorry to God, when we do not solve our problems in the best way. Guide the children in a prayer of confession as they eat each cake or cracker. Invite the children to say a simple prayer of confession to God.

Cracker #1: Think of a time when you did something that hurt someone. Tell God you are sorry for what you did. Decide how you will tell the person you are sorry, too.

Cracker #2: Think of a time when you did not stop a fight or argument between others. Tell God you are sorry for not being a peacemaker. Decide how you could have been a peacemaker in that situation.

Cracker #3: Think of a time when you did not want to do the right thing. Decide what would have been the right thing for you to do. Ask God to help you make decisions that bring peace to you, your family, and to others.

Cracker #4: Think of a time when you did the right thing in solving a problem. Thank God for helping you be a creative thinker and problem-solver. Make a promise to God that you will live God's love and be a peacemaker. As the leader, close with a verbal prayer, thanking God for the assurance of forgiveness and God's promise to help us solve our problems in God's way of peace. Or use the prayer at the bottom of this page.

3. Distribute the white embroidery threads. Have the children help each other tie the thread beside the other three colours. Explain that white is a colour that reminds us of peace. Encourage the children to thank God for creative minds to solve problems peacefully.

4. Make a Peace Promise Mural (see the illustration). Give the children the opportunity to symbolize their commitment to peace in a visible way by placing their footprints on a giant mural. Print today's memory text on a piece of newsprint or cloth (bedsheet or old tablecloth). Pour or mix poster paint in flat baking pans, large enough to hold a foot. Also have available warm, soapy water and some towels. Invite each person to make one footprint by dipping a foot into the paint and placing it on the mural. Let the children help each other wash and dry their feet. If desired, children can print their names with markers beside their footprints. Allow the mural to dry, then post it for all to see.

Dismiss the children to the next activity.

Circle Game Activity

Sometimes we expect others to do what we want. [*Pause.*] If you have been disappointed because someone has not done what you wanted, **let go of each other's hand.**

Sometimes we do not respect what others think is important. [*Pause.*] If you have not shown respect to someone, **take a step backward.**

Sometimes we hurt others by yelling, refusing to talk, or by hitting. [*Pause.*] If you have done any one of these, **turn around.**

Sometimes we do not listen carefully to others. [*Pause.*] If you have ever walked away or ignored someone, **close your eyes**.

Jesus wants us to look for what is good in others. [*Pause.*] If you have laughed at someone's joke that wasn't funny, **open your eyes and say, "Jesus is love."**

Jesus wants us to respect each other. [*Pause.*] If you have done something because it was important to another, **turn around and say, "Jesus is love."**

Jesus wants us to listen carefully to others when they say we have hurt them. [*Pause.*] If you have said you are sorry to someone, **step into the circle and say "Jesus is love."**

Jesus wants to help us be peacemakers. [*Pause.*] If you want to share God's spirit of peace with others, **join hands and say, "Jesus is love."**

Dear Jesus,

It is hard to forgive people when they hurt us and our friends. We want to hit back—and sometimes we do. But teach us to love our enemies no matter what they do. Forgive us when we do not forgive others. Help us to understand why people hurt others, and let our hearts be filled with love for them. Amen.

Session 5

David

Theme: Loving God by Showing Kindness
Bible Text: 2 Samuel 4:4; 9:1-13
Story Focus: David showed kindness and brought Mephibosheth into his home.
Faith Focus: We live God's love when we are kind, just, and generous.

Memory Texts

"You shall love the Lord your God with all your heart, and with all your soul, and with all your strength, and with all your mind; and your neighbor as yourself" (Luke 10:27, NRSV).

"'Love the Lord your God with all your heart and with all your soul and with all your strength and with all your mind'; and, 'Love your neighbor as yourself'" (Luke 10:27, NIV).

And what does the Lord require of you but to do justice, and to love kindness, and to walk humbly with your God? (Micah 6:8b, NRSV).

And what does the Lord require of you? To act justly and to love mercy and to walk humbly with your God (Micah 6:8b, NIV).

"'Speak, Lord, for your servant is listening'" (1 Samuel 3:9b, NIV and NRSV).

Beloved, since God loved us so much, we also ought to love one another (1 John 4:11, NRSV).

Dear friends, since God so loved us, we also ought to love one another (1 John 4:11, NIV).

Depart from evil, and do good; seek peace, and pursue it (Psalm 34:14, NRSV).

Turn from evil and do good; seek peace and pursue it (Psalm 34:14, NIV).

Do good, be rich in good works, generous, and ready to share (1 Timothy 6:18b, NRSV, adapted).

Do good, be rich in good deeds, be generous and willing to share (1 Timothy 6:18b, NIV, adapted).

Anticipated Outcomes

1. The children will review from memory all the previous texts as well as the verse for this session.

2. The children will learn that love for God is expressed in acts of loving-kindness.

Setting

Plan to be indoors. Be sure table space is available.

Materials

- Large heart made from red bristol board
- Coloured construction paper
- Pencils, scissors, markers, staplers
- Pieces of green embroidery thread, 20 to 26 cm., (8 to 10 in.), one per child
- Snack: a mixture of food items (vegetable or fruit pieces, dried fruit, raisins, and chocolate chips) or ice cream bars

Method

Bible Memory

As the children assemble, review the memory texts learned thus far. Learn today's text, using hand clapping, finger snapping, or clapping hands with a partner. Invite children to suggest other body movements to the verse until everyone has it memorized.

Prayer Theme

1. Make hands wreaths. Hands are a symbol of our commitment to acts of love and kindness toward everyone we meet. Ahead of time, prepare a large red heart. Have the children each trace one hand onto coloured construction paper and cut it out. They may wish to personalize their hands with decorations and/or add their name to illustrate the unique gift that each person offers to others. Staple the hands onto the heart.

Option #1: Instead of a large heart, cut out giant letters that say LOVING-KINDNESS or GOD IS LOVE and have the children staple the handprints onto the letters.

Option #2: Use fabric paint to trace around the hand onto a white cloth or pieces of lightly coloured cotton material. Ask a quilter to make this into a quilt that could be donated to a women's shelter.

Talk about the finished product. What does it tell us? Remind the children that God has made each person unique and with different gifts so that we can show God's love and kindness in our own way. The "many hands" illustrate that together we can make a difference in showing others the way God wants us to relate to people who are different. Even though our hands are all different, they all can do the same things. We are to treat all people with respect and kindness because God has made each one of us in God's image. To show our love for God, we show our love to others through acts of kindness.

2. Distribute the snack. As the children eat the food mixture, invite each person to tell one act of loving-kindness that they could do for someone very soon.

Reflection and Prayer

1. Gather into small groups of four to six. Sing together the song "Lord, Listen to Your Children Praying."

2. Distribute the green embroidery threads. Tie this last thread onto the previous ones. Explain that green represents life and growth and change. As we listen to God and talk with God, our friendship with God grows stronger and we become better persons.

3. Review together the prayers of the week and allow time for individual prayers. Encourage the children to give audible prayers if they feel comfortable doing it. As leader, invite the children to hold onto each thread as they pray. It would help if you led with a verbal prayer each time.

Blue thread: Give a sentence prayer, thanking God for something. "Thank-you, God, for...."

Yellow thread: Sit quietly in silence for one minute. Imagine yourself listening to God's voice.

Red thread: Thank God for being your friend. Make a friendship promise to God.

White thread: Ask for God's help in being a peacemaker. Sit quietly, feeling God's peace.

Green thread: Ask God to help you find one person to whom you could give a special act of kindness. Imagine doing a good deed to someone who is not a friend.

4. Sing "Lord, Listen to Your Children Praying."

5. Encourage the children to wear their prayer bracelets for the rest of the week. When they are ready to remove the bracelets, suggest that they tie knots in both ends and tape the bracelet onto the back of their "Letters to God" booklet from Session 3.

6. Join hands in one large circle. Go around the circle saying the Bible memory verse for today, phrase by phrase, until all have said it.

7. Say a prayer, asking God to help the children take what they learned with them and continue to grow in their friendship with God.

Dismiss the children to the next activity.

Bible memory passages

Pray and Learn

Sessions 1-5

"You shall love the Lord your God with all your heart, and with all your soul, and with all your strength, and with all your mind; and your neighbor as yourself" (Luke 10:27, (NRSV).

"'Love the Lord your God with all your heart and with all your soul and with all your strength and with all your mind'; and, 'Love your neighbor as yourself (Luke 10:27, NIV).

And what does the Lord require of you but to do justice, and to love kindness, and to walk humbly with your God? (Micah 6:8b, NRSV).

And what does the Lord require of you? To act justly and to love mercy and to walk humbly with your God (Micah 6:8b, NIV).

"'Speak, Lord, for your servant is listening'" (1 Samuel 3:9b, NIV and NRSV).

Beloved, since God loved us so much, we also ought to love one another (1 John 4:11, NRSV).

Dear friends, since God so loved us, we also ought to love one another (1 John 4:11, NIV).

Depart from evil, and do good; seek peace, and pursue it (Psalm 34:14, NRSV).

Turn from evil and do good; seek peace and pursue it (Psalm 34:14, NIV).

Do good, be rich in good works, generous, and ready to share (1 Timothy 6:18b, NRSV, adapted).

Do good, be rich in good deeds, be generous and willing to share (1 Timothy 6:18b, NIV, adapted).

Ideas for Memorizing Bible Passages

Sessions 1-5: Luke 10:27

New Revised Standard Version

"You shall love the Lord your God x x
with all your heart, x x
and with all your soul, x x
and with all your strength, x x
and with all your mind; x x
and your neighbor as yourself." x x

New International Version
"'Love the Lord your God x x
with all your heart x x
and with all your soul x x
and with all your strength x x
and with all your mind'; x x
and, 'Love your neighbor as yourself.'" x x

Options

1. x x can be two hand claps, two foot stomps, clap a partner's hands twice.
2. Repeat it as a litany. The leader will say lines 1 and 6. The girls can say lines 2 and 4. The boys can say lines 3 and 5. The group can say the reference together.
3. Use mime to learn the verse. Replace key words with actions and show the word rather than say it.

For example:
love [*Cross your arms in front so that each hand touches the opposite shoulder.*]
Lord your God [*Point your right finger upward above your head.*]
heart [*Make a fist with your left hand and press to your heart.*]
soul [*Place your open right palm in the centre of your chest.*]
strength [*Raise both arms to show your "muscles" in your upper arms.*]
mind [*Touch your head with your right finger.*]
neighbour [*Do a "high-five" handshake with the person on your right.*]

If you have a creative group, have the group make up hand motions for the other words, so that eventually the entire verse could be mimed.

Sessions 1-5: Micah 6:8

New Revised Standard Version
What does the Lord [*Point upwards.*]
require of you [*Point to others.*]
but to do justice, [*Stretch hands out, palms up.*]
and to love kindness, [*Cross hands over heart.*]
and to walk [*Walk on the spot.*]
humbly [*Bow your head.*]
with your God? [*Point upwards.*]

New International Version
And what does the Lord
require of you?
To act justly
and to love mercy
and to walk humbly with your God.

Options

1. Clap on each syllable.
2. Walk on the spot and do the other actions as you repeat the words.
3. Face a partner and say alternate lines along with the actions.
4. Do the actions but say the words inside your head.
5. Put the words to music or a rap beat or accompany with instruments (drum, shakers, tambourines, etc.).

Session 3: 1 John 4:11

New Revised Standard Version
Beloved,
since God loved us so much,
we also ought
to love one another.

New International Version
Dear friends,
since God so loved us,
we also ought
to love one another.

Session 4: Psalm 34:14

New Revised Standard Version

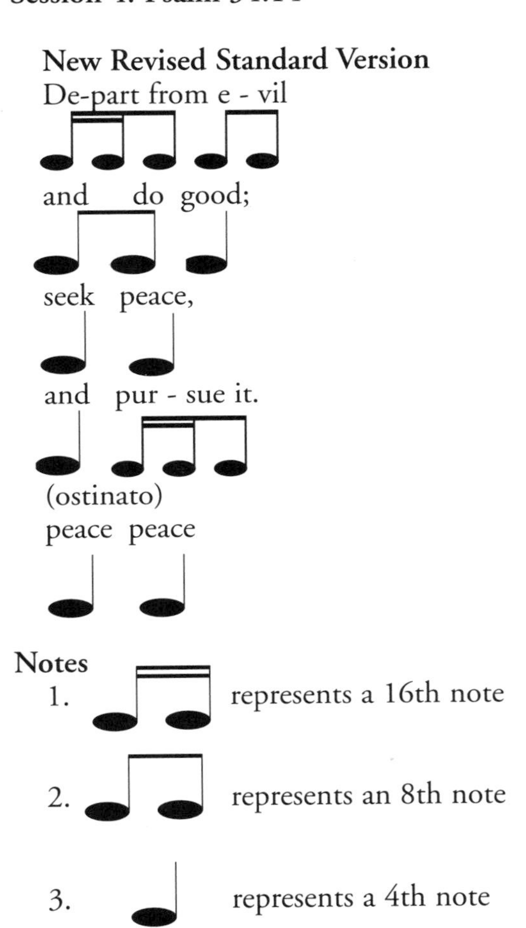

New International Version
Turn from evil
and do good;
seek peace
and pur-sue it.
peace peace

Options

1. Say the verse as a chant, using the rhythm given.
2. Chant the verse, clapping the beat.
3. Have half the group quietly repeat "peace" (ostinato) on the beat while the other half chants.

Session 5: 1 Timothy 6:18

New Revised Standard Version, adapted
Do good, x x
be rich in good works, x x
generous, x x
and ready to share. x x
1 Timothy 6:18b x x

New International Version, adapted
Do good, x x
be rich in good deeds, x x
be generous x x
and willing to share. x x
1 Timothy 6:18b x x
Note: x represents a hand clap

Options

1. Use finger snapping instead of clapping.
2. Clap a partner's hand (right palm on first clap, left palm on second).

Creative Ways to Review Memory Verses

1. Use hand motions, clapping, finger snapping, stepping, skipping, etc.
2. Say each line around the circle with each person saying a phrase. Have a contest with the clock to see how fast the verse can be said correctly when each person in turn contributes a word.
3. Repeat the verse by alternating groups. Have the girls say one line, boys another, or other groupings by colours of clothing, age, etc.
4. Repeat the verse as an echo response. The leader says each line and the group repeats it.
5. Use mime to learn the verse. Replace key words with actions that show the word rather than say it. After the group has learned the hand motions that go with the key words, repeat the verse, replacing the words with the actions. If you have a creative group, have the group make up hand motions for the other words, so that eventually the entire verse could be mimed.
6. Put the memory verse on an overhead. Use paper strips to cover the key words. Continue to cover more words until the entire verse is repeated from memory.
7. Write the words on flash cards. Distribute the cards, one per person. Have a contest against the clock to see how quickly the words are placed in order. As more verses are learned, mix the flashcards together to create a greater challenge, especially for the older children.
8. Place the flash cards on a clothesline with clothespins. Have a child remove one card while the rest of the group repeats the verse, filling in the

missing word. Continue until all the cards are off the line.

9. Form two teams. The first team says the first phrase of the verse. The second team repeats the phrase and adds the next phrase. The first team repeats the first and second phrases, then adds the third phrase. Continue until the entire verse is repeated by both teams.

10. Stand in a circle with the leader holding a ball. The leader says the first phrase, then bounces the ball to another person to continue the verse with the next phrase. If the person who receives the ball cannot continue the verse, she or he will repeat the first phrase or say "pass" and bounce the ball to another. This game is best played as a review, after the children have learned the verses quite well.

11. Write the memory verse on a blank puzzle or onto a picture that can be mounted on cardboard and cut up. Distribute the pieces and have the children discover the text, or see how quickly they can assemble the puzzle and then repeat the verse.

Make and Take Resource

Introduction

Programme

During Make and Take the children do a hands-on project that reinforces the session and overall themes. Each child will make a door or wall hanging. The hanging is completed in five sections. Each panel illustrates or symbolizes the session theme. At the end of the five sessions, the children can assemble the sections to make a personalized door hanging on felt or bristol or poster board.

Leadership

The Make and Take leader should be someone who enjoys doing craft activities. This person can give good instructions for children to follow and encourages children to work independently and creatively. The intent of this craft is to help children express the theme of loving God in a personal way through a variety of media. The finished product can be a constant reminder of God's love for the child.

The ideas given are suggestions for you as leader. Use your own creative gifts for this project, or create a new craft activity. See Leaders and responsibilities, page 12, for more ideas.

If you have a large group of children, plan to have an assistant Make and Take leader in addition to the group leaders. Give the group leaders clear instructions as to how they can assist you. Expect them to participate fully during the session. Encourage them to continue to build on the theme by talking with the children about the symbols they chose for the craft.

Preparation

Each session is designed for thirty minutes. Allow for cleanup time between groups. Be sure to dismiss your group on time.

Read through this entire resource section so you have a complete understanding of the ongoing craft activity. Collect all materials necessary for the crafts. Take the time to make a sample hanging so that you know whether or not the instructions are clear or need to be adapted. Display the completed hanging for the children.

Print a set of instructions on chart paper for easy reference by the group leaders and older children.

If you wish to substitute a craft, be sure that the replacement activity expresses the theme adequately and appropriately. See page 114 for alternate ideas.

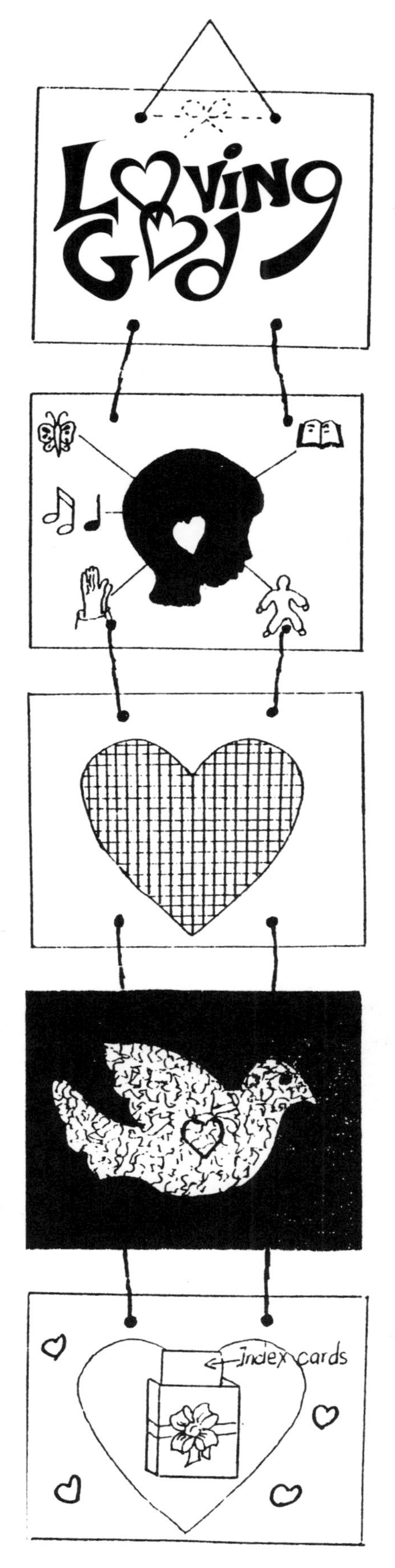

Additional craft ideas

If some children finish their panel early, have some simple craft activities available for them to do. The extra activity should be self-directed. Prepare instruction cards that the children can follow easily.

1. Make a large mural. Set up a paint corner for children to create a picture to represent the theme Loving God.
2. Put a large piece of newsprint on the wall. Provide markers and encourage children to write messages to God on a "graffiti board."
3. Some craft shops have small wooden hearts. Make necklaces with the hearts and shoelaces, or incorporate them into craft items that could be given to senior adults at a care center.

Reinforcement of the theme

Each day discuss with the children how the craft activity fits in with the theme. Invite the children to personalize each panel as an expression of their love for God.

Door or Wall Hanging

Each session the children will make a panel that will be attached with rings to the previous one. The children will use different symbols and art media to illustrate the theme of each session on a different panel. By Session 5, each child will have completed a wall hanging to remind them of the theme Loving God.

The panels can be made using coloured bristol or poster board, felt, or other cloth. Younger children will find bristol or poster board easier to work on; the older children may enjoy working with felt; or offer the choice of panel background materials. The cloth may be more expensive than bristol or poster board.

Each child will be given one panel of each of five colours: blue, yellow, red, white, and green. The colours coincide with the colours of embroidery threads that are given to the children each day in Pray and Learn (see page 85).

The bristol board (poster) panels are attached to each other with loose-leaf snap rings. If you are using felt, heavy string or yarn is required. You may wish to experiment with larger loose-leaf rings instead of string. The completed panels may be hung with string attached to the top panel (see the illustration).

The heart symbol may be used on each panel to reinforce the theme of loving God in each session's response. Encourage the children and leaders to be creative.

The wall hangings will remain in the Make and Take centre until Session 5 when they are completed. The completed wall hanging is quite large. If you wish to make a smaller hanging to save on material costs, adjust the sizes given accordingly. For instance, one could cut bristol board (poster) pieces into fourths rather than halves. Each piece would be sufficient for four children rather than two.

If there are children who can participate only part of the time, allow them to take their panels with them. You may wish to have each child take the panels home after each session and assemble the hanging at home.

Materials for paper hanging (for each child)
- One piece of bristol board or poster board (43 x 56 cm., 17 x 22 in.) of each colour: blue, yellow, red, white, and green
- Eight loose-leaf rings (3 to 4 cm., 1 1/4 in.)
- Heavy string (1m., 1 yd.)
- Specific supplies for each session's symbol (see session plans)

Materials for cloth hanging (for each child)
- One panel of felt or other cloth (43 by 56 cm., 17 x 22 in.)
- Ten pieces of dowel (61 cm., 24 in.)
- Heavy string (2 m., 2 yd.) to attach panels and to hang the completed creation
- Darning needles, scissors

To prepare felt panels

1. Cut to desired size.
2. Fold the ends over approximately 5 centimeters, (2 inches).
3. Topstitch to form a pocket for the dowel.
4. Mark spots approximately 13 centimeters, (5 inches), from the outer edge (top and bottom) for the string to be threaded through.

Optional craft activities

Board Game (Sessions 1 and 3)

Design a simple board game using themes and game ideas from the Talk and Move Resource section for Sessions 1 and 3. Children could make a game board from bristol or poster board, cardboard, wood, or styrene. Draw on squares or a course with markers. Have them draw or write in detours, obstacles, ways to avoid obstacles; make up questions for each other to answer, etc.

Encourage the children to be creative in their design, reminding them that the content and playing the game should take precedence over the final shape. If you wish to change the game board each session, have the children cover the board with clear adhesive-backed plastic. Use water-soluble markers and plastic stick-on shapes to draw the game designs.

Wooden Plaques

Use the logo pattern (page 29) to make a plaque out of wood. Invite a woodworker to coordinate and lead this activity. It may take several days to complete if the wood is to be cut, sanded, and varnished.

Food

For several sessions, this group could make food that can be used for the snack or given to others.

For Session 1, make pretzels that can be eaten in snack time during Pray and Learn. Tell the story of the pretzel. If you follow the three-way rotation schedule, you will need to have pretzels available for the first group who will not yet have had Pray and Learn. One suggestion is to make the pretzels to be given to another group. The last group will share them with other leaders, younger children, and the drama team.

Soft Pretzels

Measure out 4 cups of flour.

Add 1 teaspoon salt and 1 tablespoon fast-rising yeast.

Mix together, then add 1 1/2 cups hot tap water.

Knead the dough until smooth. Cut into small pieces. Using your hands, roll the dough into ropes and twist into pretzel shapes.

Place shapes on a lightly greased cookie sheet. Whip 1 egg. Using a pastry brush, brush egg onto the dough. Sprinkle with course salt and bake at 425 degrees for 12 to 15 minutes. Allow pretzels to cool.

For Session 3, make Friendship Cookies. Use a sugar cookie recipe to make heart-shaped cookies for a snack and to give away. Or instead of sugar cookies, prepare Rice Krispies squares, brownies, or a cake (use a cake mix and bake in two pans). Cut into heart shapes and ice before eating or sharing.

Session plans for Make and Take

Session 1

Hannah

Theme: Loving God by Praying
Bible Text: 1 Samuel 1:1—2:1-11
Story Focus: Hannah's love for God was demonstrated in her prayer life. She trusted that God would answer her prayer. She fulfilled her promise to God when she took Samuel to the temple to live with Eli.
Faith Focus: We show that we love God when we talk to God. We trust that God will hear and answer us when we pray.

Anticipated Outcome

Children will make the first panel of their hanging: the theme *Loving God.*

Materials for bristol or poster board hanging

- One blue piece of bristol or poster board for each child
- One stencil for every three children (see pattern, p. 118)
- Pencils, black markers
- White glue
- Flat paintbrushes
- Various colours of glitter or a variety of glitter glue

Method #1

Beforehand, make stencils from the copy (page 118). Use paper bags, mural paper, or bond paper to make additional stencils. Enlarge the original copy provided to cut out the letters, or use as is, depending on the size of the bristol or poster board. The piece without the letters becomes the stencil. To make stencils, stack up to five sheets of paper and cut with a very sharp Exacto knife.

Give the children stencils and the following instructions:

1. Transfer the letters onto the panel with a pencil.
2. Outline the words with a black marker.
3. Using the flat paintbrush, fill in or outline one letter at a time with white glue.
4. Sprinkle glitter on the wet glue, dumping off any excess.
5. Complete one colour before moving on to another.
6. Thread the heavy string through the top two holes and tie.
7. Print your name on the back of the panel.
8. Hang or set aside to dry.

Materials for felt/cloth hanging

- One blue piece of felt or cloth for each child
- Different sizes of letter stencils
- Pencils, black markers
- Fabric glitter paint

Method #2

1. Have available different sizes of letter stencils and encourage the children to design their own letters.

2. Follow Method #1, using fabric glitter paint instead of white glue.

3. Using the string and a darning needle, draw the heavy string through the marks at the top edge of the felt and tie. Insert the dowels.

Dismiss the children to the next activity.

Loving
God

Session 2

Samuel

Theme: Loving God by Listening
Bible Text: 1 Samuel 2:18-21, 26; 3:1-21
Story Focus: When Samuel realized that God was calling to him, he responded by listening to God's voice.
Faith Focus: We show we love God when we listen for God's voice and respond by our living.

Anticipated Outcome

The children will make the second panel of their hanging: a symbol of prayer that relates to listening to God speak.

Materials for bristol or poster board hanging

(for each child)

- One yellow piece of bristol or poster board
- One sheet of black construction paper
- Pointed scissors
- Pencils, black markers
- White glue
- Slide, film, overhead projectors or strong flashlights
- White chalk
- Listening symbols (p. 121)
- Materials to use for symbols
- Pieces of coloured yarn

Method #1

Plan to have extra adult assistance to help to trace a silhouette of each child's profile. Have enough projection equipment to accommodate groups of eight children.

1. One person at a time poses for a silhouette. Instruct the children to sit

between the beam of the projector light and the wall to get a side profile that fills a 23 x 30-centimeter, 9 x 12-inch, sheet of black construction paper that is taped to the wall.

2. An adult will trace around the profile of the silhouette, using a piece of white chalk.

3. Each child cuts out her or his own profile with sharp scissors.

4. Glue the profile in the centre of the bristol or poster board piece.

5. Glue a red heart in the ear position of the silhouette.

6. Arrange the other listening symbols on the bristol or poster board (see illustrations).

7. If you wish, glue pieces of yarn from the symbols to the heart.

8. Give each child two loose-leaf rings to attach to the Session 1 panel.

9. Set aside.

Materials for felt/cloth hanging (for each child)

- One piece of yellow felt
- One piece of paper (23 x 30 cm., 9 x 12 in.)
- One piece of black felt (23 x 30 cm., 9 x 12 in.)
- A variety of pieces of coloured felt (8 x 8 cm., 3 x 3 in.) for symbols
- Sharp scissors
- White glue
- Listening symbols (p. 121)
- Materials to use for symbols
- Pieces of coloured yarn

Method #2

1. Follow instructions for the silhouette as given in Method #1, steps 1-5. It is not necessary to use black paper for the silhouette pattern.

2. Using the cutout silhouette as a pattern, trace onto felt piece with white chalk, and cut out again.

3. Glue the felt silhouette onto the yellow felt panel.

4. Make symbols of coloured felt, shaped yarn, or other fabric materials and glue onto the felt as in Method #1.

5. If desired, knot a coloured yarn piece, and using the darning needle, thread it from the symbol through the heart. Knot or glue the thread at the back.

6. Attach the two felt pieces at the marks, using string and darning needles. Insert dowels and set aside.

Dismiss the group to the next activity.

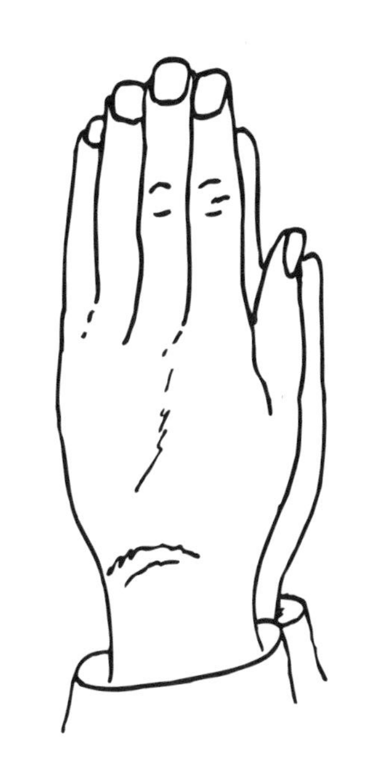

Session 3

Jonathan

Theme: Loving God by Loving Others
Bible Text: 1 Samuel 20:1-42
Bible Background: 1 Samuel 18 and 19
Story Focus: Jonathan risked his life for his best friend, David, though it meant danger for him.
Faith Focus: We show that we love God when we are a true friend.

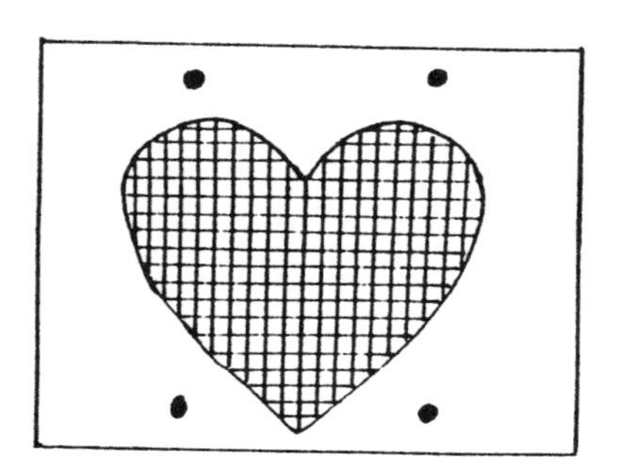

Anticipated Outcome

Children will make the third panel of their hanging: a heart to symbolize our friendship and love for God.

Materials for bristol or poster board hanging

(for each child)

- One red piece of bristol or poster board
- One sheet of white construction paper (23 x 30 cm., 9 x 12 in.)
- 14 strips of red or pink stiff ribbon (1-2 cm., 1/2 in., width) cut in 36 cm., 14 in., lengths
- Scissors
- White glue

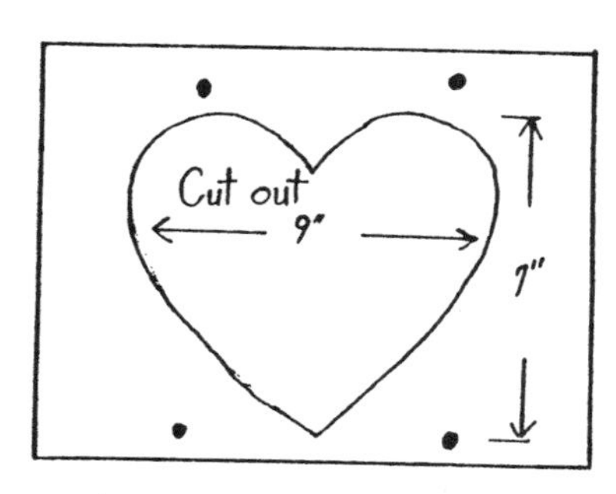

Method #1

1. Cut a 23 x 18 centimeters, (9 x 7 inches), heart out of the centre of the red bristol or poster board. It might be helpful to prepare a cardboard pattern for the younger children to trace the heart onto the board.
2. Cut vertical slits 1 to 2 centimeters, (1/2 inch), apart in the sheet of white construction paper. Prepare these ahead of time for younger children. Cut several layers, using an Exacto knife. Older children can do their own cutting.
3. Weave the strips of ribbon through the white construction paper slits (see illustration).

4. Using white glue, mount the completed woven sheet behind the cutout heart of the bristol or poster board.

5. Attach the panel to the Session 2 panel, using two loose-leaf rings.

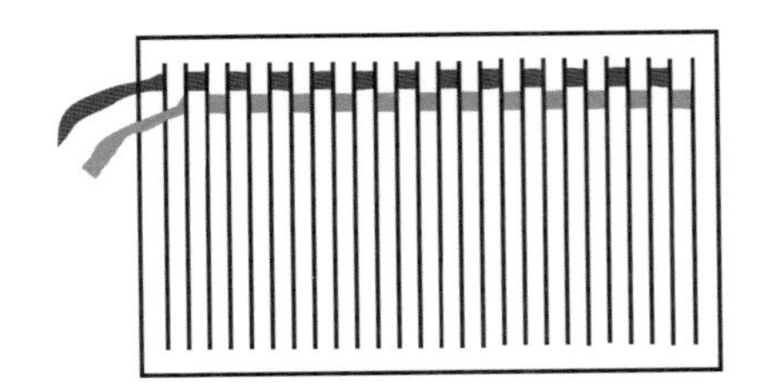

Materials for felt/cloth hanging (for each child)

- One piece of red felt
- One piece of stiff Pelon (23 x 30 cm., 9 x 12 in.)—i.e., interfacing that is **not** iron-on—or white construction paper
- Wallpaper knife or Exacto knife
- A piece of corrugated cardboard
- 25 strips of red or pink ribbon (1 cm., 1/4 in.) cut 36 cm., 14 in., in length

Method #2

1. Use the same instructions as in Method #1. Allow the older children to cut their own strips in the Pelon.

2. Place the Pelon on the cardboard. Using the knives carefully, cut slips vertically.

3. Weave the ribbon carefully through the slits (see illustration). Encourage the children to be creative in their weaving.

4. Attach the panel to the previous one, using darning needles and string.

5. Insert the dowels and set aside.

Dismiss the children to the next activity.

Session 4

Abigail

Theme: Loving God by Making Peace
Bible Text: 1 Samuel 25:1-38
Story Focus: Abigail demonstrated creative thinking skills in order to keep peace between two enemies, Nabal and David.
Faith Focus: We show our love for God when we solve our problems in peaceful ways.

Anticipated Outcome

Children will make a peace dove for their fourth panel: a symbol of God's peace.

Materials for bristol or poster board hanging

- One piece of black bristol or poster board for each child
- Eggshells (broken into large pieces) or pieces of coloured tissue paper
- Some eggshells coloured with red food colouring
- Peace symbol stencils (p. 126)
- Chalk
- White glue (tacky glue works best)
- Flat paintbrushes

Method #1

1. Make several copies of the peace stencil (page 126), using mural, butcher paper, newsprint paper, or brown paper bags. Enlarge the stencil or use as is, depending upon the size of your board. Using an Exacto knife, it is possible to make five stencils at a time. There should be one stencil for every three children. Give the children the following instructions:

1. Cut out the inside part of the stencil.
2. Trace the stencil onto black bristol or poster board with chalk.
3. Apply glue with the flat brush to a small portion of the dove.

4. Quickly stick on the eggshells to form the mosaic design. Place red eggshells in a heart shape, either inside the dove or on the bristol or poster board. Or instead of eggshells, tear tissue paper into small pieces, place a piece on the end of a pencil, stick into the glue, and attach to the bristol or poster board.
5. Attach the panel with loose-leaf rings to the previous panel. Set aside.

Materials for felt/cloth hanging

- Black felt
- Eggshells (broken into large pieces) or pieces of coloured tissue paper
- Some eggshells coloured with red food colouring
- Peace symbol stencils (p. 126)
- Chalk
- White glue (tacky glue works best)
- Flat paintbrushes

Method #2

1. Follow instructions for Method #1. Use felt instead of bristol or poster board.
2. Encourage the older children to design their own peace symbol.
3. Include the red heart somewhere in the panel.
4. Attach the panel with two string loops, using darning needles.
5. Insert dowels and set aside.

Dismiss the children to the next activity.

Session 5

David

Theme: Loving God by Showing Kindness
Bible Text: 2 Samuel 4:4; 9:1-13
Story Focus: David showed kindness and brought Mephibosheth into his home.
Faith Focus: We show that we love God when we are kind, just, and generous.

Anticipated Outcomes

Children will complete their hangings: a gift box to symbolize their willingness to show loving-kindness as a response to God's love.

Materials for bristol or poster board hanging

(for each child)

- One piece of green bristol or poster board
- One piece of red construction paper (23 x 31 cm., 9 x 12 in.)
- One gelatin box (135 g., 3 oz.)
- Gift wrapping paper, ribbons, bows of all shapes and colours
- Transparent tape
- White glue
- Small index cards (at least five per child)
- Markers, pens, pencils
- Scissors

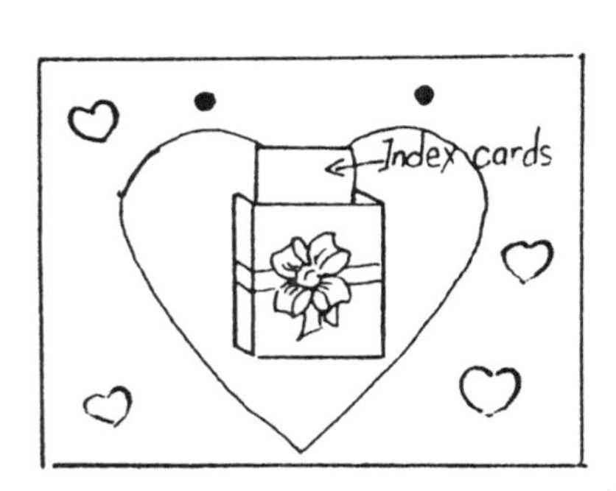

Method #1

1. Cut off one end of the gelatin box, approximately 1.25 centimeters., (1/2 inch), from the end.
2. Have each child wrap and decorate her or his box, using ribbons, bows, etc.
3. Using white glue, attach the box to the middle of the bristol board.

4. Cut out hearts from red construction paper, one for each recipient of a coupon. Glue the hearts around the box.
5. Complete the coupons. On an index card, write or draw an act of loving-kindness that you are willing to do for a family member, friend, neighbour, etc.
6. Slip the coupons into the open end of the gift box.
7. Complete the hanging by attaching this panel to the previous one with the last two snap rings.

Materials for felt/cloth hanging

- A piece of green felt for each child
- Red felt for various shapes of hearts
- One gelatin box (135 g., 3 oz.) for each child
- Gift wrapping paper
- Ribbons and bows of all shapes and colours
- Transparent tape
- White glue
- Index cards (at least five per child)
- Markers, pens, pencils
- Scissors

Method #2

1. Follow instructions as for Method #1. Use green felt panels.
2. Attach the panel to the previous one, using a darning needle and string.
3. Insert dowels to complete the wall hanging.

Dismiss the children to the next activity.

Early Childhood

Introduction

Programme

Use this curriculum for children ages four and five—pre-kindergarten and kindergarten age levels. Children who have completed kindergarten are part of the main curriculum, pages 33-128, but could be part of this programme if it were adapted to meet their needs.

Loving God with Heart and Hands expresses more fully the *Loving God* theme for this age. The children will learn about five Old Testament characters who loved God and showed their love for God in different ways:

1. Hannah showed her love for God by praying and talking to God.
2. Samuel showed his love for God by listening when God spoke to him.
3. Jonathan showed his love for God by loving his friend, David.
4. Abigail showed her love for God by being a peacemaker.
5. David showed his love for God by being kind to others.

As you prepare to teach this curriculum, take the time to read the Scripture texts and to think about the Faith Focus given in each session. Think about the meaning of the story for your own life and for the lives of the children in your care. Pray for the time you will be spending with the children; pray for the children. Pray that you will express your love for God in your actions with the children.

Outline

This programme is designed for sessions of two and three-quarter hours each. See page 133 for a suggested schedule format. The length and order of the sessions may be altered to suit your particular needs. Some activities may need to be omitted if your programme is shorter. Younger children may require more playtime while older children could use more "talk" time.

Gather (15 minutes in small groups)

Collect the children's offering, talk about the offering project, distribute name tags, take attendance, conduct group-building activities, etc.

Worship (30 minutes in one large group)

All of the four- and five-year-olds meet together for singing, introducing, and reviewing the memory verses, and listening to the Bible story.

If you choose to have the Early Childhood group with the older children (kindergarten through grade 8), remember that the Worship has been planned for the older children. Your younger children may feel overwhelmed, confused, or anxious trying to fit into the Worship with the older children.

1. Tell the Bible story. Each session contains a Bible story written for this age. One person can be your storyteller for the week. Suggestions are given with each story for ways to add variety and include participation by the children.

2. Sing and pray. The music coordinator, or teachers, may lead the singing part of the Worship. The theme song is "Love, Love," page 175. Other songs are found on page 176 and in the Worship Resource section, pages 54-60. Include familiar songs each session.

Group Activities (60 minutes in small groups)

Children are together in their small groups with one or two leaders. Relationships are built as the children play games related to the themes, work on a project together, eat a snack, retell the Bible story, and learn a Bible verse. If you wish, divide this time in half, interspersing these activities with the centres (see page 132).

1. Play games. Familiar or simple games have been adapted that will reinforce the session theme. These games are meant to help all the children feel included. They are not too competitive.

2. Work together. These activities provide a practical hands-on approach to the theme. The children work in a small-group setting.

3. Share a snack. Snacks are listed each session, keeping the session theme in mind. You may choose to use the same snacks as the older children. Ask the Loving God coordinator for a listing of snack items.

4. Retell the story. Children will best remember the stories if they have a chance to put them in their own words. Brief suggestions are given for ways to get the children started. The younger children may need more suggestions. As an option, tape or videotape the story as it is being told during story time. Replay it for the children to re-enact during retell time. Do not use tapes for the original story. A "real" personal story has more meaning.

5. Memorize the Bible verse. The verses for each session are introduced during Worship.

Session 1: Say the verse eight times, emphasizing (and jumping up) a different word each time, e.g., **God** will always help us when we pray; God **will** always help us...."

Session 2: I [*Point to self*] will listen [*Point to ear*] to what God [*Point upwards*] the Lord [*"L" with fingers starting at chest*] will say [*Point to mouth and away*].

Session 3: This [*Index finger in hand*] is my commandment [*Open hands like a Bible*] that you love [*Cross hands on heart*] others [*Hands point outward*].

Session 4: Have the children form a line like a train by holding each other's elbows. Say the verse in rhythm while moving arms and walking: "Peace I leave with you, my peace I give to you."

Session 5: Clap an even rhythm while repeating the verse: "Share what you have and be generous."

Centres (50 minutes in a large group)

One or two small groups (up to twenty children) meet together. The teachers and helpers divide up the responsibilities for the activities listed for this session. One leader should prepare and guide the craft activities; another could supervise the mobil, books, and tapes, etc. The children may rotate in groups to each activity or choose which order they prefer.

Centres (use in rotation)

1. Mobile. This craft adds a symbol each day to a hand pattern (see page 138). The completed mobile is taken home after Session 5.

2. Take-home craft. Each day, directions are given for a craft that will remind children of the theme for the session. This craft can go home with the child on the day it was made. The cost of the centrepiece for Session 5 is minimal.

3. Special activities. These activities need some preparation by an adult but should not need much supervision, with the exception of Session 5.

4. Books/tapes. Suggested books are listed on pages 167-168. If you do not have a teacher available to read stories during Centres time, consider taping the story ahead of time. Have simple tape recorders on hand. A few children may gather around the book and listen to the text on tape. Taping a story is not meant to replace the book, but it allows flexibility for leaders and encourages independent learning for the children. When taping, remember to include a special sound to alert the children to turn the page.

5. Toys. An assortment of toys suitable for group play may be made available as one centre. Use puzzles, building toys, dress-up clothes, cars, dolls, etc.

6. Colouring. Provide crayons or markers and pictures from a purchased colouring book. Have on hand paper for creative artwork, too. Such a centre requires little supervision.

Closing (10 minutes in a large group)

Use this time as a quiet time to review the theme of the day. Puppet plays are written for each session. Conclude the session with singing and/or saying the closing blessing (see page 30).

Puppet plays

Five plays are included that work with a simple puppet theatre such as a table turned on its side. Encourage three youth or adults to rehearse and present the short plays for each session. Three sheep, a dog, a shepherd, and a bear are the puppets needed as well as a few props that are listed with each play. See pages 169-174 for the puppet plays.

Groupings

If your group is large, divide them into several groups each with a teacher and helper. Groups can have four- and five-year-old children in each group or be separated by ages. If possible, keep the groups small for more personal interaction. No group should have more than ten children.

To identify the groups for instructions, rotation activities, and fun, give group names using colours. Name tags can be made using bristol or poster board cut in the shape of a heart. Heart-shaped balloon bouquets of the different colours can identify the gathering place for the children.

Master schedule

SESSION	Session 1	Session 2	Session 3	Session 4	Session 5
THEME	• Loving God by Praying	• Loving God by Listening	• Loving God by Loving Others	• Loving God by Making Peace	• Loving God by Showing Kindness
GATHER • Attendance • Offering	• See general information, p. 130				
WORSHIP • Bible story • Prayer • Singing	• Hannah (repeat prayers) • See songs, pp. 54-60	• Samuel (listening actions)	• Jonathan (adults act out parts)	• Abigail (movable figures)	• David (act out with props
GROUP ACTIVITIES 1. Play Games	• *Name Tick Name Game Hanging:*	• *I hear with my little ear.* • *Animal groups* • *Sam Says*	• *Frisbee toss* • *Ducks, Ducks, Geese*	• *Problem-solving games*	• Puzzle • Relays
2. Work together	• Prayer time	• Work project	• Hands wreath	• Peace march	• Make and serve cookies
3. Share a snack	• Pretzels	• Noisy snack	• People cookies	• Giant cookies, apples, oranges	• Cookies or ice cream
4. Retell the story	• Act out with props	• Children tell story	• Children act out	• Children act out	• Children act out
5. Memorize the Bible verse	• God will always help us when we pray (Psalm 46:1, paraphrased).	• I will listen to what God the Lord will say (Psalm 85:8a, NIV).	• This is my commandment, that you love others (John 15:12, paraphrased).	• Peace I leave with you; my peace I give to you (John 14:27, NRSV).	• Share what you have and be generous (1 Timothy 6:18, paraphrased).
CENTRES 1. Mobile	• Praying mouth	• Listening ear	• Loving heart	• Hugging arms	• Helping feet
2. Take-home craft	• Stained-glass window	• Walkie-talkies	• David and Jonathan dolls	• Peace pennants	• Table Centrepiece
3. Special activities	• Prayer • Collage	• Listening activities	• Paper-plate Frisbees	• Add-a-smile picture	• Personalized sandals
4. Books/ tapes	• See Resources, p. 139, for books	• See Resources, p. 149, for books	• See Resources, p. 154, for books	• See Resources, p. 159, for books	• See Resources, p. 165, for books
5. Toys	• See p. 132	• See p. 132	• See p. 132	• See p. 132	• See p. 132
6. Colouring	• See p. 132	• See p. 132	• See p. 132	• See p. 132	• See p. 132

Session titles and themes

Session 1

Hannah

Theme: Loving God by Praying
Bible Text: 1 Samuel 1:1—2:1-11
Story Focus: Hannah's love for God was demonstrated in her prayer life. She trusted that God would answer her prayer. She fulfilled her promise to God when she took Samuel to the temple to live with Eli.
Faith Focus: We show that we love God when we talk to God. We trust that God will hear and answer us when we pray.
Bible Memory Verse: God will always help us when we pray (Psalm 46:1, paraphrased).

Session 2

Samuel

Theme: Loving God by Listening
Bible Text: 1 Samuel 2:18-21, 26; 3:1-21
Story Focus: When Samuel realized that God was calling to him, he responded by listening to God's voice.
Faith Focus: We show that we love God when we listen for God's voice and respond.
Bible Memory Verse: I will listen to what God the Lord will say (Psalm 85:8a, NIV).

Session 3

Jonathan

Theme: Loving God by Loving Others
Bible Text: 1 Samuel 20:1-42
Bible Background: 1 Samuel 18 and 19
Story Focus: Jonathan risked his life for his best friend, David, even though it meant danger for him.
Faith Focus: We show that we love God when we are a true friend.
Bible Memory Verse: This is my commandment, that you love others (John 15:12, paraphrased).

Session 4

Abigail

Theme: Loving God by Making Peace
Bible Text: 1 Samuel 25:1-38
Story Focus: Abigail demonstrated creative thinking skills in order to keep peace between two enemies, Nabal and David.
Faith Focus: We show that we love God when we solve our problems in peaceful ways.
Bible Memory Verse: Peace I leave with you; my peace I give to you (John 14:27, NRSV).

Session 5

David

Theme: Loving God by Showing Kindness
Bible Text: 2 Samuel 4:4; 9:1-13
Story Focus: David showed kindness and brought Mephibosheth into his home.
Faith Focus: We show that we love God when we are kind, just, and generous.
Bible Memory Verse: Share what you have and be generous (1 Timothy 6:18, paraphrased).

Session plans for Early Childhood

Session 1

Hannah

Theme: Loving God by Praying
Bible Text: 1 Samuel 1:1—2:1-11
Story Focus: Hannah's love for God was demonstrated in her prayer life. She trusted that God would answer her prayer. She fulfilled her promise to God when she took Samuel to the temple to live with Eli.
Faith Focus: We show that we love God when we talk to God. We trust that God will hear and answer us when we pray.
Bible Memory Verse: God will always help us when we pray (Psalm 46:1, paraphrased).

Gather

1. Take attendance. Have the children put their names or pictures of things they like to eat onto the bulletin board.

2. Play a simple get-to-know-you game, such as the *Name Game*. Say, "My name is _________, and I like to eat ________." Go around the circle, having the child fill in the blanks. The whole class repeats each line: "Her/His name is _______, and he/she likes to eat_______."

If the children really enjoy this game, you may try doing all the statements around the circle without stopping. Then, if they need a challenge, go around the circle in the opposite direction.

3. Talk about what you are going to be doing during the session. If you have chosen a group name, talk about its meaning. This is also a good time to talk about rules and expectations.

4. Collect the offering and talk with the children about the project. Use visual aids if possible.

Worship

1. Learn the last line of each prayer that is said during the story. [*Thank-you, God, for listening to me.*] Have a signal such as a bell to let them know when

to say the line. Practice saying this with the children so that when they hear the bell in the story, they will be ready to repeat it with you.

2. Tell the Bible story:

This is a story about Hannah and her husband, Elkanah. They didn't have any children. Hannah often wished that they would have a baby. Sometimes she would cry when she was so sad and lonely. Hannah and Elkanah often went to their church that was called a temple. They went to the temple together, because they both loved God very much. At the temple, they liked to pray to God. When they were praying, it was just like God was right there in the room with them. They were talking to a friend. They would tell their friend, God, about the things they liked to do. They told God about how they were feeling. Sometimes they had exciting things to tell God. They even told God about the things that made them sad.

One day Hannah was especially sad about not having any children in their family. She was standing by herself in the corner and crying quietly. She told God how sad she was. God could hear her saying, "God, you are very special, and I love you very much. I'm so sad and lonely without any children. Please let me have just one baby. Then I will be happy. And, God, there is one more thing. If you give me a baby, in a few years I will bring the child to the temple to be your special helper. [*Thank-you, God, for listening to me.*]

God heard Hannah praying, even though she was talking very quietly. Hannah felt better after she talked to God. Soon it was time for Hannah and Elkanah to go back home. After many months, Hannah did have a baby boy. She and Elkanah named him Samuel. Hannah was very happy. She liked holding baby Samuel and feeding him and rocking him to sleep. Hannah remembered to say "thank-you" to God for her baby. God could hear her say, "God, you are my friend, and you have made me very happy. Thank-you for this special baby boy that you have given to us. [*Thank-you, God, for listening to me.*]

Hannah also remembered the promise she had made to God that when Samuel was old enough, she would take him to the temple to be a helper. Soon Hannah and Elkanah were ready to go to the temple.

This time they brought Samuel along with them. He met someone who lived and worked at the temple. He was a priest—that's like our ministers or pastors today. The priest's name was Eli. He was very old and couldn't see very well. He could certainly use a helper like Samuel. Samuel was still a little boy, but there were many things that he would be able to do to help at the temple. Hannah always remembered to thank God for her son, Samuel. Even when Samuel was helping at the temple, she loved him very much. She was glad that he could be God's special helper. Hannah always remembered to say [*Thank-you, God, for listening to me*].

3. Pray: "Thank-you, God, that Hannah could talk to you. Thank-you for hearing Hannah's prayer. Thank-you, God, that I can talk to you, too. I'm glad that you listen to me just like a friend. [*Thank-you, God, for listening to me. Amen.*]

4. Sing favourite songs (see pages 175-176).

Group Activities

1. Play games.

Name Tick: It tags one person and says his/her name; that person must then respond by saying It's name. To make the game easier, everyone may help out with the names.

Name Game: Even if you did play this game during attendance time, it would also work well now.

Guess Who: It says, "I know someone who is wearing ________." The children guess who It is thinking of. Then that person along with It can hop or run around the circle together.

2. Work together. Share in prayer time:

Option 1: Using the names or pictures on the bulletin board from attendance time, guide the children in a prayer time, saying a sentence together for each person represented. An example might be, "God, Susie likes apples; thank-you for apples." This is very similar to the prayer collage during Centres time, and can be used as an introduction or follow-up to that activity.

Option 2: Consider the four parts of prayer (show accompanying pictures).

Part 1. Adoration. Say: "I love you, God, because...." [*Cross hands over heart*].

Part 2. Confession. Say: "I'm sorry for...." [*Kneel*].

Part 3. Thanksgiving. Say: "Thank-you, God, for...." [*Lift hands*].

Part 4. Supplication. Say: "Please help me...." [*Open hands*].

Make up prayer sentences using these actions to symbolize the different types of prayer. Have the children choose one kind, do the appropriate action together, and take turns finishing the sentence prayer.

Some ideas to get you started:

"I love you, God, because..." (you made kittens, you are special, you love me).

"I'm sorry for..." (yelling at Joey, taking the ball away from Sarah).

"Thank-you, God, for..." (friends, sunshine).

"Please help me..." (to make a new friend, to do what you want me to do).

3. Share a snack. Choose soft or hard pretzels; the shape is a symbol for prayer. As you eat the snack, tell this story about the pretzel:

The pretzel is made in the shape of crossed or praying arms. When they were first made a long, long time ago, they were called "little arms" because people would cross their arms over their chest to pray to God. Church leaders gave little pretzels to children to help them remember to say their prayers. When you are finished eating your pretzel, fold your arms like a pretzel and say a thank-you prayer to God for the snack.

4. Retell the story. Have children act out the story using props (baby doll, dress-up clothing).

5. Memorize the Bible verse: God will always help us when we pray (Psalm 46:1, paraphrased). See page 108 for ideas.

Centres

1. Mobile. Add a symbol each day. The children may take it home at the end of the week. The first day will need more individual attention as children learn skills to be used the rest of the week.

Teacher

- Precut the hand and mouth shapes from fun foam (or bristol or poster board) for each child (see patterns, pages 140-141).

- Punch appropriate holes in fun foam.
- Have ready 2 1/2 chenille stems (or pipe cleaners) and five beads per child.
- Bend one chenille stem in half, forming a loop; wrap 1/2 chenille end around loop to secure (this makes loop for hanging).

Children

- Thread each of three ends of looped chenille into centre hand holes.
- Add a bead to each end.
- Bend chenille over each bead to secure.
- Thread one end of last chenille into thumbhole of hand.
- Slip bead onto end of chenille, above hand.
- Bend chenille over bead to secure.
- Thread last chenille into hole of mouth shape.
- Slip bead onto end of chenille, bending to secure.

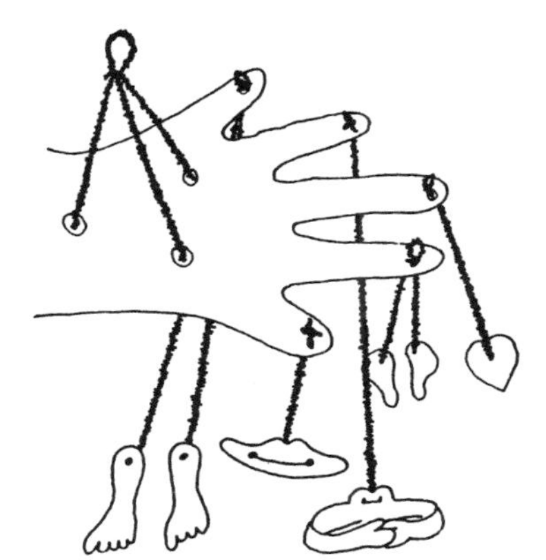

2. Take-home craft. Make Stained-glass Windows. This craft will remind the children of the Bible story and the memory verse.

Teacher

- Photocopy window frames and temple activity page for each child (pages 144-145).
- Punch a hole in the top corners of window frames (page 144).
- Cut lengths of yarn or ribbon (35 cm., 14 in.) for each child.
- Precut window shapes (page 145).

Children

- Colour the shapes.
- Glue the shapes onto the matching shape on the window frame (page 144).
- Thread yarn through the holes in the top of frames for hanging.

Teacher

- Tie knots in the yarn to hold it in place.

3. Special activity. Make a prayer collage. This can be a form of a prayer for the child, as the child tells God what he or she is thankful for when a picture is glued onto the paper.

Teacher

- Cut many pictures out of magazines that remind children to be thankful.
- Have ready some glue and one piece of paper per child.

Children

- Choose pictures of things for which he or she is thankful, and glue onto paper. (You may choose to talk about these pictures later.)

4. Books/tapes. Use these ideas or select other appropriate titles.

- *What Can I Say to You, God?* Verses from the Psalms on Prayer. Elspeth Campbell Murphy, illustrated by Jane E. Nelson (David C. Cook, 1980).
- *Everybody, Shout Hallelujah!* from David and I Talk to God Series (author and publisher same as above).
- *I Can Talk with God,* Helen Caswell (Nashville, Abingdon Press, 1989).

5. Toys. See page 132. Encourage the children to play with age-appropriate toys.

6. Colouring. See page 132.

Closing

See page 30.

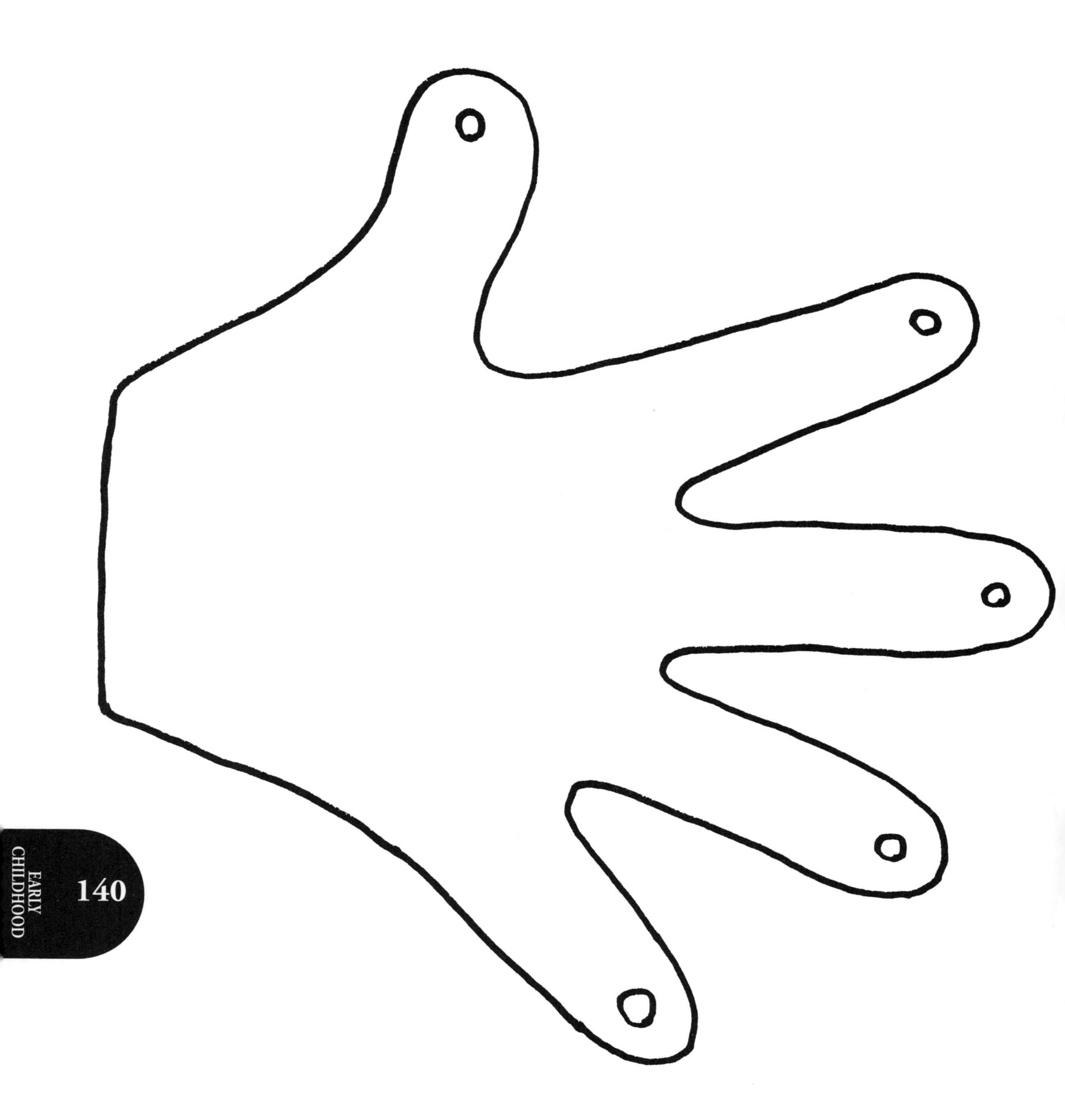

Permission is granted to purchasers of this curriculum to photocopy this page for use with the Loving God *curriculum.*

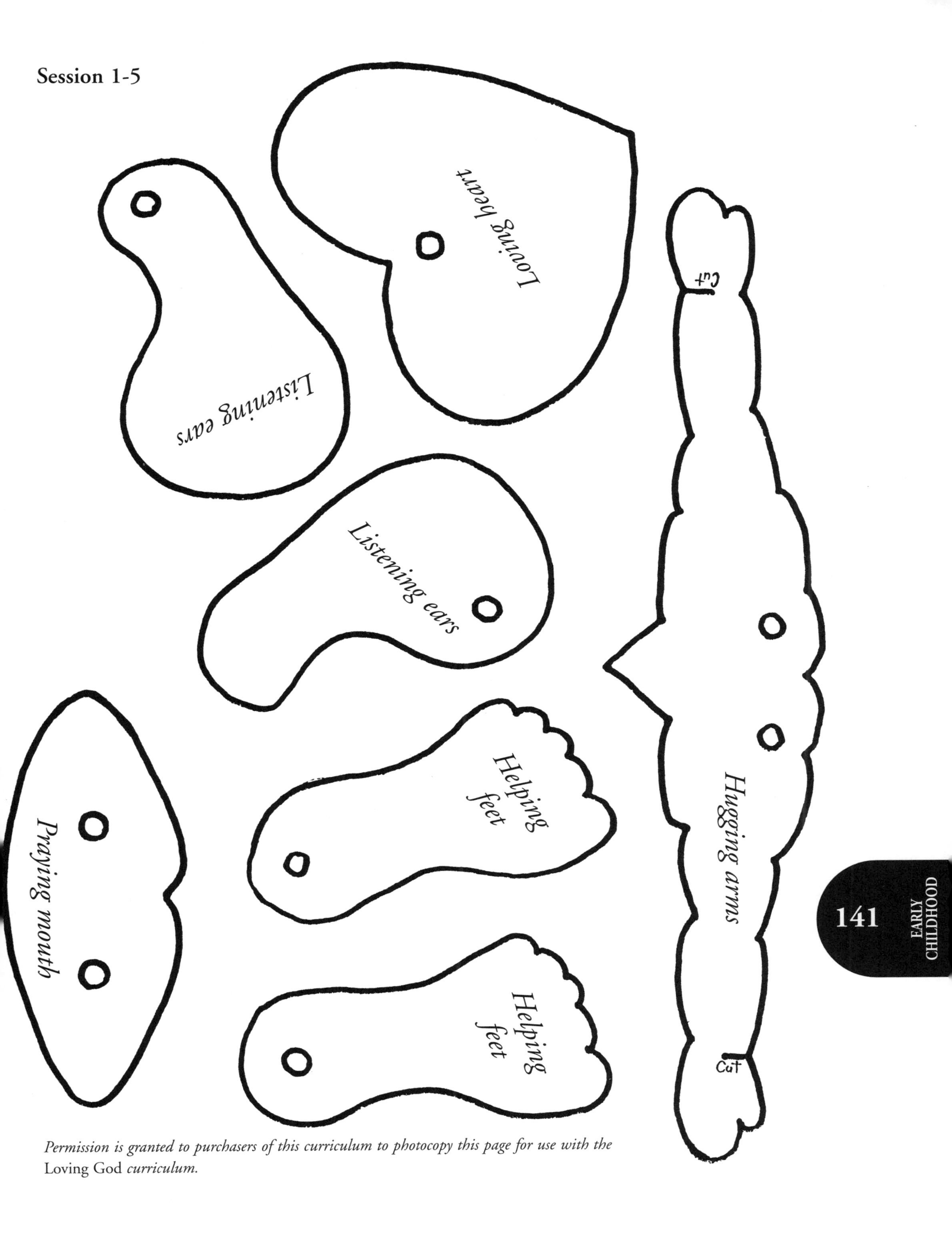

Permission is granted to purchasers of this curriculum to photocopy this page for use with the Loving God *curriculum.*

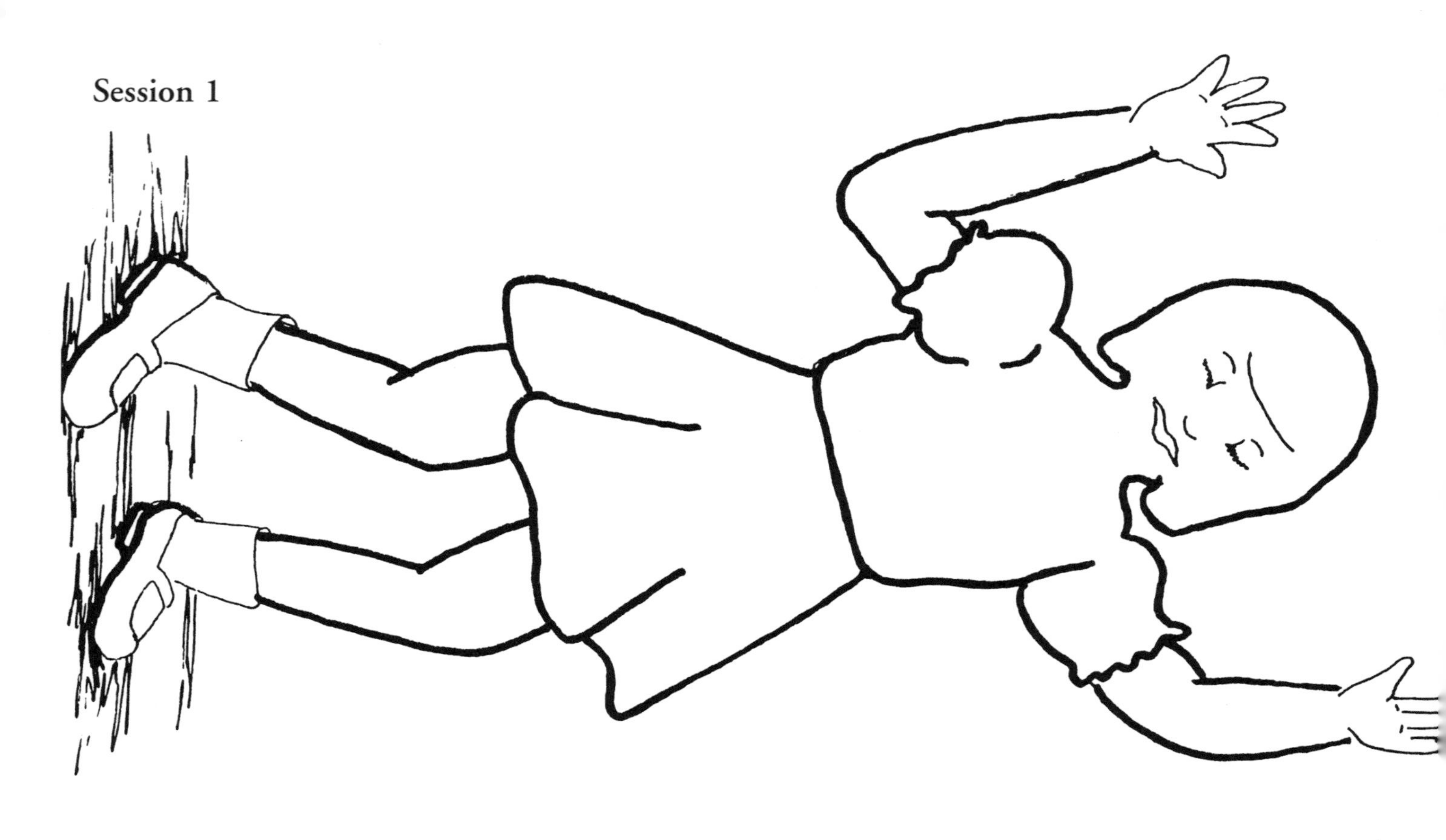

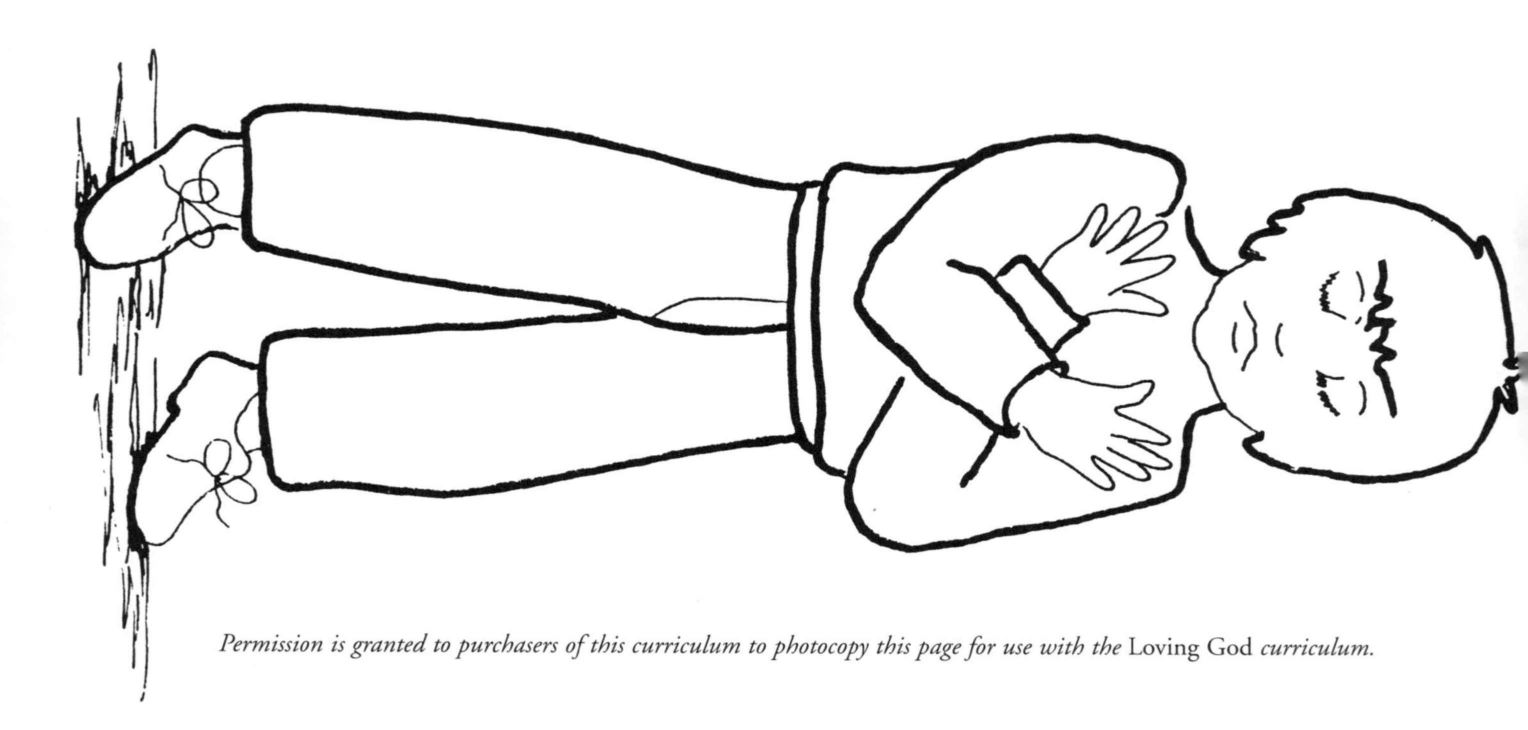

Permission is granted to purchasers of this curriculum to photocopy this page for use with the Loving God *curriculum.*

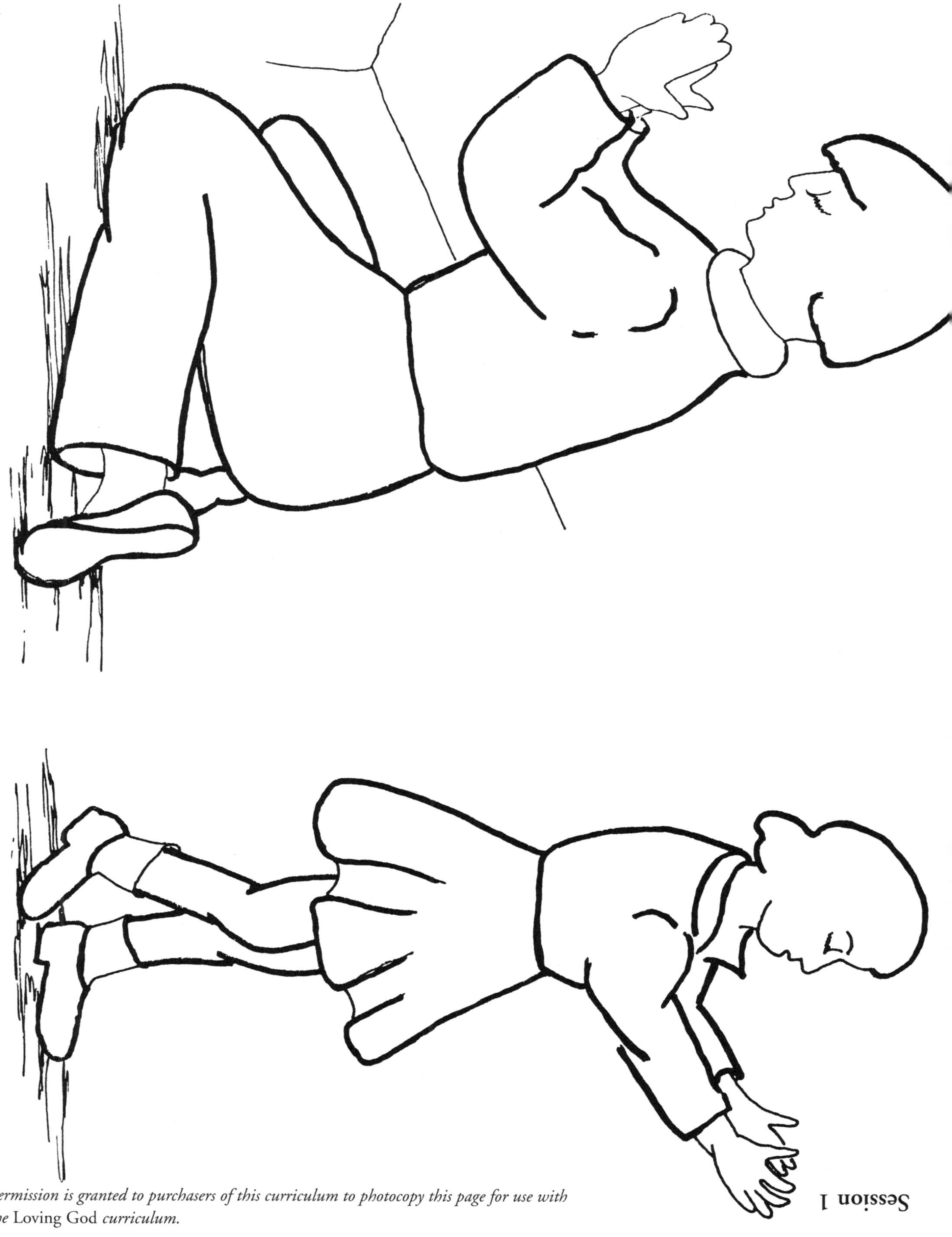

Permission is granted to purchasers of this curriculum to photocopy this page for use with the Loving God *curriculum.*

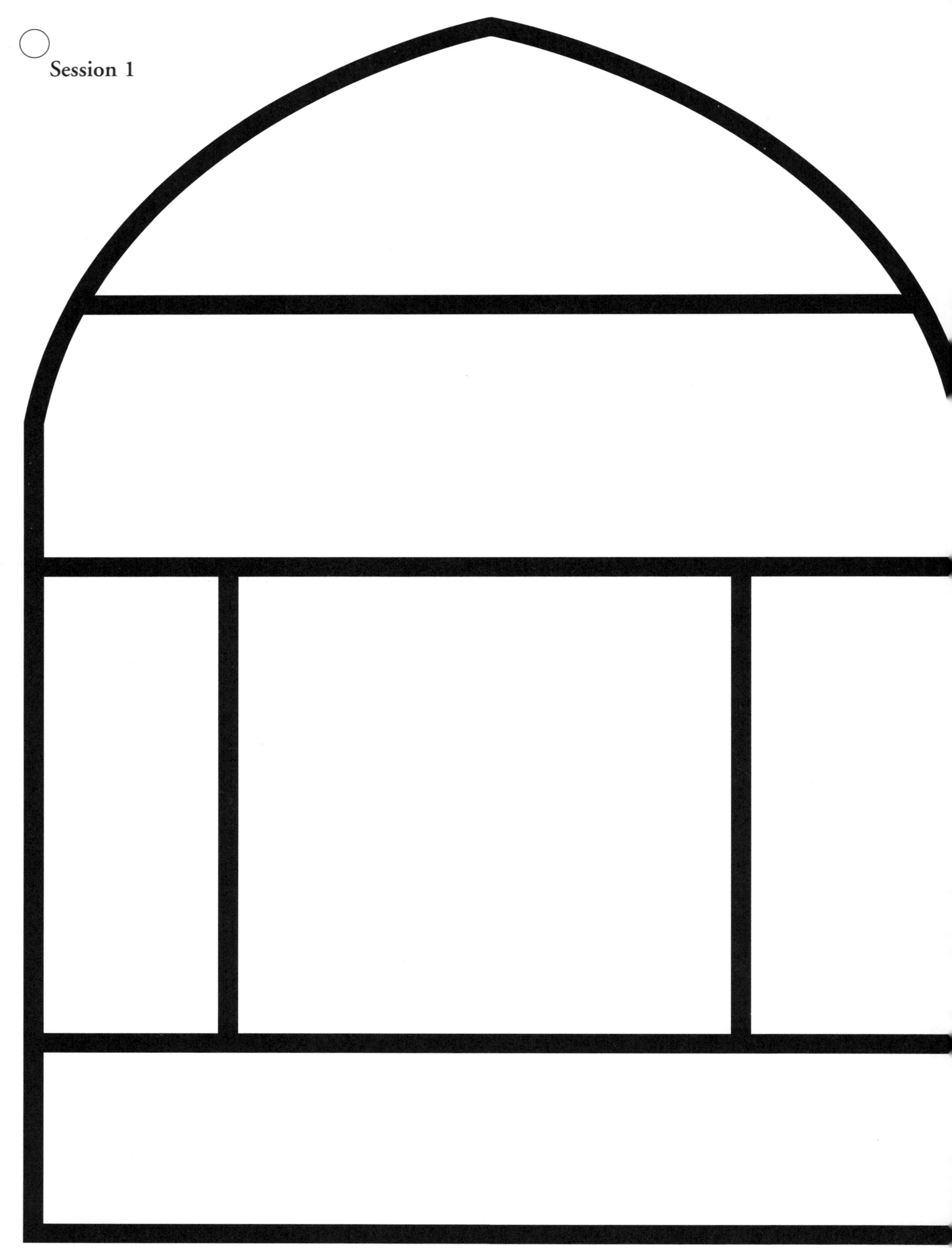

Permission is granted to purchasers of this curriculum to photocopy this page for use with the Loving God *curriculum.*

God will always help us when we pray.

Psalm 46:1

[Per]mission is granted to purchasers of this curriculum to photocopy this page for use with the Loving God *curriculum.*

Session 2

Samuel

Theme: Loving God by Listening
Bible Text: 1 Samuel 2:18-21, 26; 3:1-21
Story Focus: When Samuel realized that God was calling to him, he responded by listening to God's voice.
Faith Focus: We show that we love God when we listen for God's voice and respond.
Bible Memory Verse: I will listen to what God the Lord will say (Psalm 85:8a, NIV).

Gather

See page 130.

Worship

While telling today's story, do appropriate actions with the children as marked. (*)

1. Tell the Bible story:

Yesterday we heard a story about Hannah who prayed to God. Hannah had a baby named Samuel. When Samuel was a boy about your age, he was a helper at the temple. Today we are going to hear more about what Samuel did at the temple.

Samuel was getting bigger all the time. Now he was just about your age and he could do lots of things to help old Eli. Eli lived at the temple, and Samuel was right there to help him all the time. In the morning he might help Eli to make the beds. He could pull the blankets up neatly. Let's all do that together too. (*)

Then they would eat breakfast and wash the dishes together. (*) Next they might clean the temple, picking up and making sure things were in their proper place. (*)

On some days Eli would bring out the special brass candlesticks. Samuel could see that they were not nice and shiny anymore so he would get out a soft cloth to polish them, like this. (Show candlesticks, if possible, and polish them.) (*)

Samuel would open the big wooden doors, (*) so the people could come into the temple to pray and talk to God.

After lunch, when the dishes were cleaned up again, (*) Samuel would sweep the floor. (*)

Maybe in the afternoon, Samuel and Eli would go outside and work in the garden and water the flowers and vegetables. (*)

Then it would be time to set the table for supper. (*) Samuel could stir the pot of soup that they had made. (*)

No more people were coming to the temple now. It was time to close the big wooden doors. (*)

It was getting dark. Samuel could help put oil in the lamp (*) so that Eli could light it.

In the evening Eli would sometimes tell stories to Samuel, and they both enjoyed this time together. Samuel liked helping Eli at the temple, but now he was tired and ready to go to bed. (*)

One night Samuel said his prayers and climbed into his own small bed. He put his head down on his pillow. (*)

Eli was in the next room in his big bed. Samuel closed his eyes (*) and was almost asleep. Then he thought he heard someone call his name. (**hand to ear*)

He opened his eyes, looked around, and thought, *Eli must need me.* So he jumped up, (*) ran (**in place*) to Eli.

Samuel said, "Here I am; you called me."

Eli said, "I didn't call you. Go back and lie down." So Samuel went back to bed. (*)

Just as he was closing his eyes again, (*) he heard, "Samuel." He jumped up again (*) and hurried to Eli. (*)

Samuel said, "Here I am; you called me."

Eli said, "No, Samuel, I didn't call you; please go back to bed."

Samuel did as he was told and put his head back down on the pillow (*) and started to close his eyes again. (*)

Samuel thought that Eli was playing tricks on him. Then he heard the voice again saying, "Samuel!" He opened his eyes. Samuel didn't know that it was God who had been calling him.

He jumped up, (*) ran to Eli, (*) and said, "Here I am; you called me."

Eli knew all about God, and he remembered how God can talk to people in many different ways. He said to Samuel, "It must be God calling you. Go back and lie down, and if God calls you again, say, 'Talk to me, God, I'm listening.'"

So, once more Samuel went to bed. Sure enough, God called, "Samuel."

This time Samuel answered God and said, "Talk to me, God, I'm listening." So God talked to Samuel, and Samuel listened to God, just like he was in the room with him. God told him that he liked the way Samuel was helping in the temple and that there would be many more ways that he could help God as he grew bigger. Samuel liked listening to God. Samuel tried to do what God wanted.

1. Pray: "Dear God, thank-you for talking to Samuel. Thank-you that Samuel was a good listener and a good worker. Help me to be a good listener and a good worker too. Amen."

2. Sing songs (see pages 175-176).

Group Activities

1. Play games.

Outdoor games

I Hear with My Little Ear. It thinks of a noisy object and says, "I hear with my little ear something that sounds like this________." Children and teacher guess the sound, then everyone pretends to be that object. For example, say "tweet, tweet" for a bird; "vroom" for a truck (*drive the truck*); "ring, ring" for a telephone (*talk on the phone*). The teacher may have to whisper suggestions to It.

Animal Groups. Teacher whispers the name of an animal to each child, having at least three or four of each animal. Children make the appropriate sound for their animal and try to find the rest of their group by listening to the animal sounds.

Simon/Sally Says. Encourage the children to listen carefully as they play this familiar game, but do not eliminate children if they make a mistake.

Indoor games

Musical Spots. Place large pieces of newspaper "spots" on the floor. When the music stops, the children run to a spot. Take away a spot each time, but do not eliminate children. Eventually, they all crowd onto the spot that remains.

2. Work together. Just like Samuel helped in the temple, find a simple way of letting your children do a work project at church; e.g., wash windows, clean up trash around yard, plant flowers or bulbs, sweep the floor.

3. Share a snack. Have a crunchy or noisy snack. Ask the children to listen as they eat.

4. Retell the story. Have the children retell the story. The order of events is not important for the first part of the story. More guidance may be needed in the part where Samuel hears God's call.

5. Memorize the Bible verse: I will listen to what God the Lord will say (Psalm 85:8a, NIV).

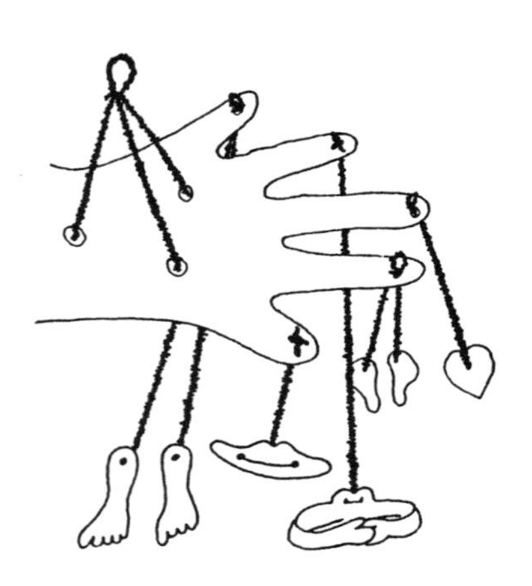

Centres

1. Mobile. The symbol for today is ears. Add them to the second finger of the hand.

Teacher

- Precut two ears per child out of fun foam.
- Punch a hole at the top of each ear.
- Have ready two chenille stems and three beads per child.

Option: Punch hole in bottom of each ear and have ready two 8-centimeter, 3-inch, pieces of chenille stems and four beads for earrings.

Children

- Attach one end of both chenille stems to second finger of hand, using bead to secure.
- Thread the other end of one chenille stem through one ear hole, and secure with bead.
- Repeat with second chenille stem.

Option: Slip one bead onto each chenille stem; bend each stem to form small circle; attach circle to bottom of each ear; and secure with additional bead to attach earring.

2. Take-home craft. Make walkie-talkies that can be taken home and played with later. Encourage the children to have fun listening to others.

Teacher

- Have ready two yogurt containers (175 g, 6 oz.) per child.
- Punch small hole in centre of container bottom.
- Have ready gimp or string (a meter or a yard length) per child.

Children

- Thread the end of gimp through the hole in each container so that the bottom surfaces of containers face each other.

Teacher

- Tie knot in each end of gimp inside the containers.

Children

- Decorate containers with felt, paper, or stickers.
- Find a friend and talk back and forth. One person speaks into the container while the other listens.
- Take turns talking and listening. Make sure the gimp is pulled tightly.

3. Special activities. Do a listening activity to help children be aware of sounds that they may or may not hear every day.

Instructions for the teacher

- Make the following sounds into tape recorder to coincide with the pictures on the Game Board (see page 150): musical instrument, smoke detector, car horn, alarm clock, toaster popping up, scissors cutting, popcorn popping, water running, baby crying.
- Instructions may be added to beginning of tape: "Listen to the sound and put a button on the picture that looks like what you hear."
- Have ready a number of game boards and buttons (nine per card). A group of children may play at the same time.

Children

- Listen to the sounds and put a button on the picture that looks like what you hear.

4. Books/tapes. Choose these or other appropriate titles:

- *The Night There Was Thunder and Stuff,* by Cynthia, art by Margaret Vouladakis (Winfield, B.C., 1993).
- *I'm Listening, God,* by Elspeth Campbell Murphy (David C. Cook).

5. Toys. See page 132.

6. Colouring. See page 132.

Closing

See page 30.

Game Board
Listening Activity
Session 2

Permission is granted to purchasers of this curriculum to photocopy this page for use with the Loving God *curriculum.*

Session 3

Jonathan

Theme: Loving God by Loving Others
Bible Text: 1 Samuel 20:1-42
Bible Background: 1 Samuel 18 and 19
Story Focus: Jonathan risked his life for his best friend, David, even though it meant danger for him.
Faith Focus: We show that we love God when we are a true friend.
Bible Memory Verse: This is my commandment, that you love others (John 15:12, paraphrased).

Gather

See page 136.

Worship

To tell the story, have three adults or youth act out the parts of Jonathan, David, and King Saul. A boy could help at the end also. Some suggestions are given throughout the story. Simple costumes might include a crown for King Saul and look-a-like T-shirts for Jonathan and David.

1. Tell the Bible story:

Our story is about two very good friends. Their names were Jonathan and David. [*Bow together.*] They loved each other very much. Jonathan's father was the king. His name was King Saul. [*Tip crown or bow to children.*] Jonathan and David were almost like brothers. In fact, David lived at the palace with Jonathan and King Saul.

Jonathan and David went almost everywhere together. [*Walk a few steps, shoulder to shoulder.*] They ate together at the king's table [*Spoon up food together*], and they shared secrets with each other. [*Whisper behind hands.*] Jonathan and David were best friends. [*Put arms around shoulders.*]

There was only one problem, but it was a big problem. Jonathan's father, the king [*Bow*], didn't like David. [*King shakes head.*] In fact, he was so angry with David that he wanted to hurt him.

David knew that King Saul wanted to hurt him, so he talked to Jonathan about it. [*Jonathan and David "talk" silently to each other.*] Jonathan didn't believe him at first, so he decided to find out for sure from his father. This wasn't very easy to do. If the King found out, he might get angry with Jonathan and hurt him, too. But Jonathan loved his friend David very much and would do anything he could to help keep him safe.

So, Jonathan and David made a secret plan. [*Put finger to their lips.*] They didn't tell anyone else about it. If they got caught, the king would be very angry.

They decided that David would go and hide [*No actions until next paragraph.*] If King Saul noticed that David was missing and didn't get angry, then David could come back to the palace. If the king did get angry, then Jonathan would know that the king wanted to hurt David. Then Jonathan could warn David so that his friend would be safe.

The two friends set their plan into action. David went to their special place to hide. [*David hides in view of the children, but to side of room.*] He didn't even come to the palace for meals. [*Rubs stomach.*]

King Saul noticed that there was an empty place at the table and asked Jonathan where David was. [*Saul questions Jonathan.*] Everything was going just as planned. Jonathan told his father that David had gone away to visit his brothers. [*Point away.*]

Jonathan didn't have to wait long to see how angry the king was. [*Saul shows his anger.*] This meant danger for David. Quickly, Jonathan went close to where David was hiding. [*Go towards David.*] He went to shoot some arrows at a target. [*Pretend to shoot arrows in David's direction.*] He took a boy along with him to chase after the arrows. [*Boy may do actions that follow in the story.*]

Jonathan shot the arrows and told the boy, "Go, find the arrows. They are far away." The boy found the arrows and took them back to the palace. [*Pick up arrows from beyond David and go back toward palace.*] David heard the secret message to go far away.

He was very sad. He knew that now he must go far away so that he would be safe from King Saul. He also knew that he probably would not see his best friend, Jonathan, again for a long, long time.

Jonathan and David cried as they waved good-bye to each other for the last time. [*Wave to each other.*] Jonathan was glad that he could help his friend, even though it had been dangerous for him, too.

2. Pray: "Thank-you, God, for Jonathan and David. They were special friends. Thank-you for keeping them safe. Thank-you for my friends, too. Amen."

3. Sing songs (see pages 175-176).

Group Activities

1. Play games. The games for today encourage the children to play with another child. Younger children might find this a new experience. Try these games.

Frisbee Toss. Using the Frisbees made during Centres time, choose a friend to play with, taking turns throwing and chasing the Frisbees.

Ducks, Ducks, Geese. Add a twist to this favourite game by having children play in pairs, holding hands while running and choosing two people who are sitting next to each other to chase you. Encourage children not to run faster than their partner. It takes cooperation to play this way.

2. Work together.

Hands Wreaths. This is a group project to be displayed in a prominent place for children to see for the rest of the week. If possible, display the wreath in the church for the next few weeks.

Teacher
- Take a picture of the whole class, using a polaroid or other camera.

Note: You may wish to take a picture on day 1 so that it can be developed by day 3.
- Have ready paint shirts, a basin of soapy water, and a towel.
- Prepare a large sheet of white paper by drawing a wreath shape.
- Leave enough space in the centre to add the class picture.
- Have ready tempera paints in a shallow pan large enough to hold a child's hand.

Children
- Put on a paint shirt.
- Dip the palm of one hand into the paint, and make a handprint somewhere on the wreath.
- Wash and dry your hands.

Teacher
- When handprints are dry, attach the class picture to the centre of the wreath.
- Display the picture.

3. Share a snack. People-shaped cookies remind the children of the two friends, Jonathan and David. Make cookies ahead of time, using gingerbread-shaped cookie cutters.

4. Retell the Bible story. Have children act out the story, telling as much of the story themselves as they can.

5. Memorize the Bible verse: This is my commandment, that you love others (John 15:12, paraphrased). Talk about the word "commandment." It is like a rule that God wants us all to do.

Centres

1. Mobile. Today's symbol is a heart. Add it in the same manner as in previous sessions.

Teacher
- Precut heart out of red fun foam.
- Punch hole in top of heart.
- Have ready one chenille stem per child and one bead.

Children
- Wrap chenille around a pencil to form a spiral.
- Attach one end of chenille to third finger of hand, using a bead to secure.
- Thread the other end of chenille through the heart and twist the end around chenille (or use bead) to secure it, so the heart hangs down.

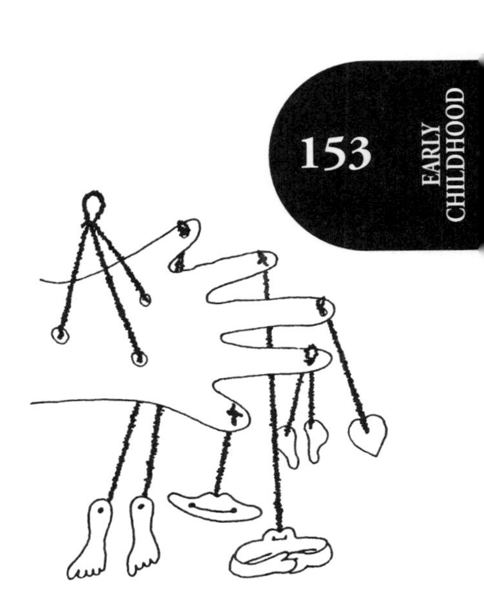

2. Take-home craft. Make Jonathan and David dolls. These dolls take advance preparation. Ask some grandparents to help out.

Teacher

- Precut and sew two dolls per child, leaving an opening on one leg for stuffing.
- Sew or glue a small piece of Velcro onto one doll's left hand and the other doll's right hand.
- Have stuffing ready. Use quilt batting, fabric scraps, beans, or other soft material.

Note: A glue gun is the quickest way to close the stuffing hole. It must be used with extreme caution.

Children

- Stuff both dolls.

Teacher

- Close the stuffing hole, using a glue gun or hand stitches.

Children

- Glue hair and facial features onto each doll, using craft glue.

3. Special activities. Make some of the following:

Frisbees—these Frisbees are easy to make and can be used later during games either inside or outside.

Teacher

- Have ready two inexpensive paper plates per child.
- Have ready glue and brushes.
- Have markers or stickers to decorate Frisbees.

Children

- With top of plate facing down, apply glue to flat part of plate bottom.
- Place bottom of second plate on top of glued plate. Press down to hold in place.
- Decorate as desired.

Postcard—this optional activity may be taken home and sent to a friend.

Teacher

- Print a message on postcard-size sturdy paper (or index card), leaving room for an address.

Children

- Paint. Sponge paint or colour the front of postcard.
- Take the card home and mail it to a friend.

4. Books/tapes. Choose from these or other appropriate titles:

- *Frog and Toad Are Friends*, Arnold Lobel (HarperCollins, 1970). The story entitled "The Letter" is appropriate.
- *Days with Frog and Toad*, Arnold Lobel (HarperCollins, 1979). The story "Alone" is appropriate for this day's theme.
- *The Short Tree and the Bird That Could Not Sing*, Dennis Foon, pictures by John Bianchi (Groundwood/Douglas and McIntyre, 1986). This is a story of a special friendship.
- *The Rat and the Tiger*, Keiko Kasza (G.P. Putnam's Sons, 1993).
- *Are You My Friend?* Janice Derby, illustrated by Joy Dunn Keenan (Herald Press, 1993).
- *The Trouble with Tuffy* is a book and tape about two children from "Agapeland" who encounter a tough boy and who put "operation kindness" into effect. Some singing is included.

5. Toys. See page 132. Encourage children to share as they play together.

6. Colouring. See page 132.

Closing

See page 30.

Cut four per child.

Permission is granted to purchasers of this curriculum to photocopy this page for use with the Loving God *curriculum.*

Session 4

Abigail

Theme: Loving God by Making Peace
Bible Text: 1 Samuel 25:1-38
Story Focus: Abigail demonstrated creative thinking skills in order to keep peace between two enemies, Nabal and David.
Faith Focus: We show that we love God when we solve our problems in peaceful ways.
Bible Memory Verse: Peace I leave with you; my peace I give to you (John 14:27, NRSV).

Gather

See page 136.

Worship

To tell the story, use flannelgraph or other figures to which you have access. Attach flat figures to cardboard tubes with paper clips or tape. "Walk" figures around on small table at children's eye level as you tell the story. Figures needed: Nabal, Abigail, David, David's workers, swords and weapons, food, and gifts.

1. Tell the Bible story:

Nabal and his wife, Abigail, were very rich. They had lots of goats and sheep. Abigail was smart and very beautiful. Nabal was mean and not very friendly.

A man named David was living close to where Nabal and Abigail lived. David wanted to become friends with his neighbour, so he sent some of his workers to meet Nabal. David told his workers what to say and do when they met Nabal. David's workers had always been kind to Nabal's workers. They wanted to be nice when they came for a visit.

David's workers met Nabal and said, "Hi, how are you today? We hope you are doing well. Long life to you." Then they said, "David wants to be friends with you. We like your workers. David wants you to like us and be nice to us, too.

Nabal answered, "I don't know David, and I certainly don't plan to be nice to him. Why should I want to be friends with him?"

David's workers went back to David and told him what had happened. David didn't like what Nabal had said. It made him angry. He wanted to fight with Nabal. David and his workers got ready to have a big fight.

Nabal's workers had heard how mean Nabal had been to his visitors. They didn't like the way Nabal had treated the visitors. They were afraid that David would be angry and would come back to hurt them all. They went to talk to Abigail, Nabal's wife. They told her what had happened.

Abigail didn't want any fighting. She worked very quickly to find a way to stop the fighting before it even started. She brought gifts and food for David and his workers.

As soon as she saw David, she said, "I'm sorry for the mean things Nabal said to you. Please listen to me. I don't want you to fight with him. Fighting is not the best way." Abigail gave her gifts to David and waited to see what he would do.

David was glad that Abigail had come to meet him, and he said to her, "Thank-you for talking to me today. I wanted to fight with Nabal. God must have sent you here to keep us from fighting. I won't fight with Nabal because you asked me not to fight." Abigail was a peacemaker that day.

2. Pray: "Dear God, thank-you for Abigail. Thank-you that she was a peacemaker. Thank-you that David listened to her and didn't fight. Help me to be a peacemaker, too. Amen."

3. Sing songs, pages 175-176. Add other favourites.

Group Activities

1. Play games.

Problem-solving game. This activity encourages children to role-play and practice solving problems. The younger children may need more guidance and suggestions for this activity. Only one activity is listed here so that you can take time to play with the objects listed below.

Teacher

- Have pictures ready that show problems, or have objects that symbolize a problem. Then play with the objects.
- Talk about the problem, and encourage children to think of ways to solve the problem.

Note: Pictures or objects might include:

- One ball and three children who each want to play with it.
- A puzzle that fell on the floor and no one wants to put it together alone.
- Two children each want to play their favourite game (a timer might be handy).
- Only three apples and everyone wants one (have a knife on hand).
- Six giant cookies on a plate at snack time and no one wants to be left out.

Be creative, yet fair.

2. Work together. Using the peace pennants made in Centres, go for a walk around your building. Sing a simple peace song like "Love, Love, Love" by Lois Brokering (*Becoming God's Peacemakers*, Newton, Kans: Faith & Life

Press, 1992, p. 133). Use the words "you and me" together in one verse. Explain that we want other people to know that we think peace is important.

Note: This song could work well at the end of Centres when pennants are finished and all of the groups are together.

3. Share a snack. Have giant cookies that need to be cut in half, use apples or oranges from the problem-solving game, or incorporate the snack into the game activity.

4. Retell the story. Have the children act out what is happening as you retell it. Encourage the children to say things by asking them questions like "What happened next?" or "Then what did he or she say?"

5. Memorize the Bible verse: Peace I leave with you; my peace I give to you (John 14: 27, NRSV).

Centres

1. Mobile. Today's symbol is hugging arms. Add them in the same manner as previous sessions.

Teacher
- Precut the arm shapes from the fun foam.
- Punch holes as shown in the pattern (page 141).
- Have ready one chenille stem per child and two beads.

Children
- Attach one end of the chenille stem to the fourth finger of the hand, using a bead to secure (see illustration).
- Attach the other end of the chenille stem to arm piece, using a bead to secure.
- Bend arms to look like they are hugging.

2. Take-home craft. Make Peace Pennants. These pennants may be used for the peace march listed in Group Activities. However, it may work best to have the march with the whole group right after Centres.

Teacher
- Photocopy page 160, "I am a Peacemaker," one per child.
- Cut the page into two pennants. Each child will need one pennant.
- Have ready markers or crayons, tape, and glue.
- Have ready one piece of construction paper cut in half diagonally per child.
- Have ready one dowel (36 cm., 14 in.) per child.

Children
- Colour the letters.
- Glue the letter page to a piece of construction paper.
- Tape construction paper to the dowel.

3. Special activities. Make an "Add-a-Smile" picture, page 161. Use this activity to remind children to help others and to become involved in peace-making each day.

Teacher
- Photocopy page 161, one per child.
- Have ready pieces of yarn (5 cm., 2 in.) for smiles.
- Have ready crayons for colouring.

Children

- Look at the picture and decide what is missing from the third picture in each row (a smile).
- Glue a yarn smile in place.
- Colour the pictures.

4. Books/tapes. Use the following titles or find others that are appropriate to the theme:

- *Days with Frog and Toad*, Arnold Lobel (HarperCollins, 1979). The stories, "The Kite" and "The Hat" fit into this theme.
- *Children's Problem Solving Series* by Elizabeth Crary (Parenting Press/Raincoast Books). These books help to raise children's awareness of ways to resolve social conflict:
    - *I Can't Wait* (How can Luke get a turn on the trampoline?).
    - *I Want to Play* (How can Danny find someone to play with?).
    - *My Name Is Not Dummy* (How can Jenny get Eduardo to stop calling her a dummy?).
    - *I Want It* (What can Amy do when Megan has the truck she wants?).

5. Toys. See page 132.

6. Colouring. See page 132.

Closing

Follow your closing ritual.

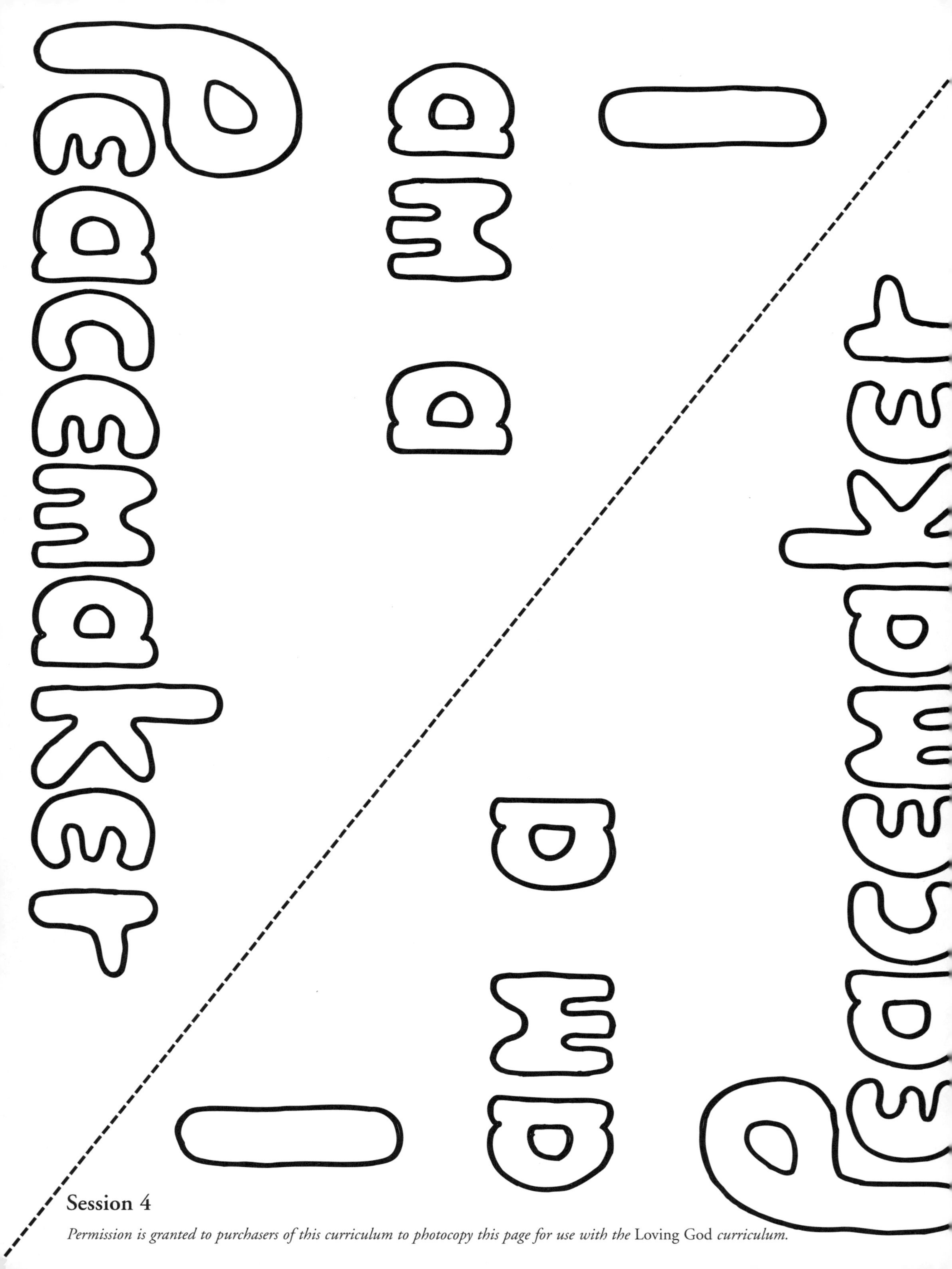

Permission is granted to purchasers of this curriculum to photocopy this page for use with the Loving God *curriculum.*

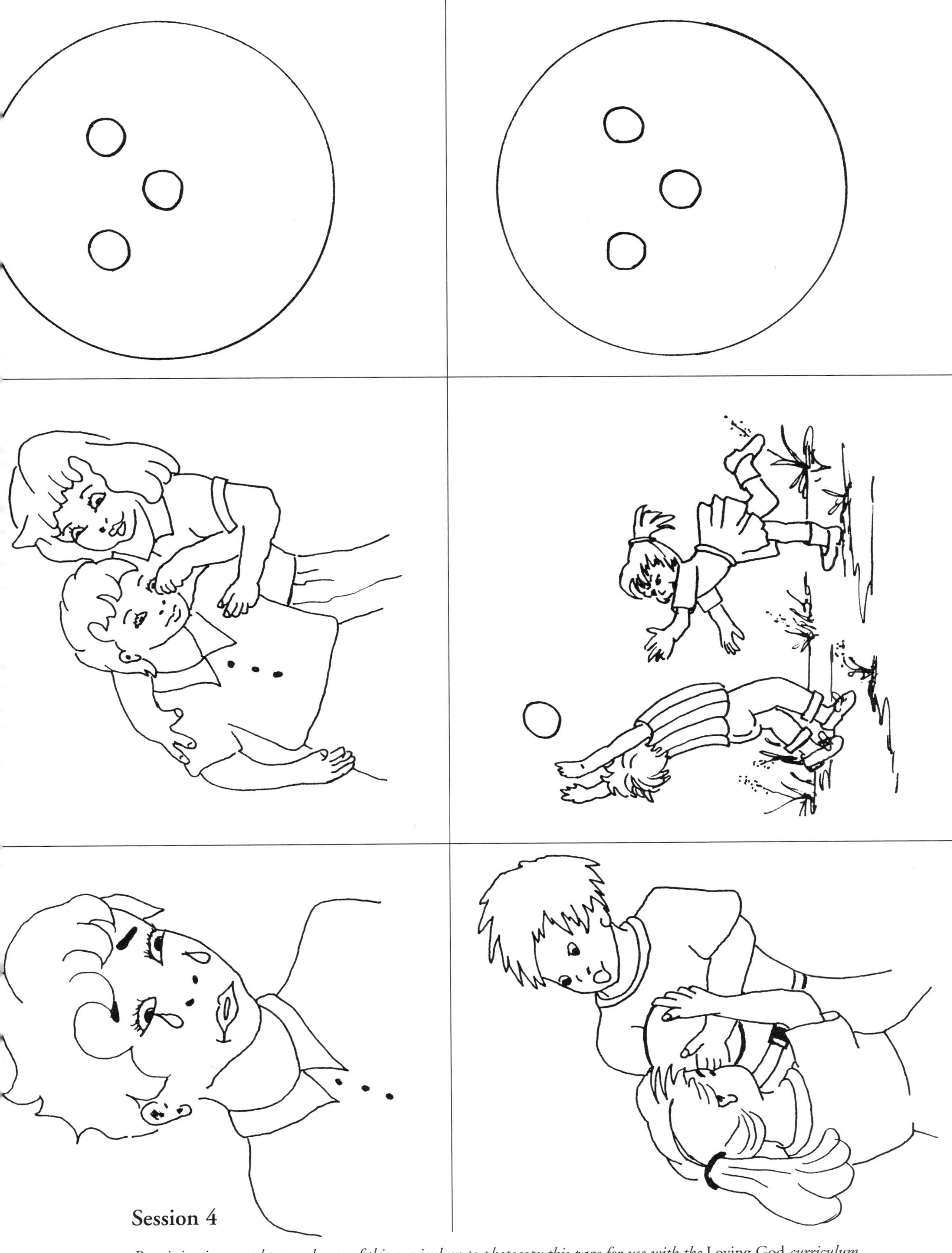

Session 4

Permission is granted to purchasers of this curriculum to photocopy this page for use with the Loving God *curriculum.*

Session 5

David

Theme: Loving God by Showing Kindness
Bible Text: 2 Samuel 4:4; 9:1-13
Story Focus: David showed kindness and brought Mephibosheth into his home.
Faith Focus: We show that we love God when we are kind, just, and generous.
Bible Memory Verse: Share what you have and be generous (1 Timothy 6:18, paraphrased).

Worship

To tell the story, use three characters: David, Ziba, and Mephibosheth. Add a few props: a table at the children's eye level set with a tablecloth, candlesticks, and a bowl of plastic fruit. Mephibosheth might be carried in on a chair to sit at the table.

1. Tell the Bible story:

Our story is about David. You probably remember him from another story this week. This time David has become the king. He still remembers King Saul and his good friend Jonathan. King David is at his palace.

David was a very kind person, even though he was the king. He had much more than he needed, so he wanted to do something kind for someone else.

One day while he was sitting at his table, he said to Ziba, one of the servants, "Isn't there anyone around here to whom I can be kind?"

Ziba said, "I'm sure you remember your old friend Jonathan. He had a son named Mephibosheth who can't walk. He can't work as a farmer because he can't walk. He doesn't have a way to earn money. I think there would be something you could do for him."

So David invited Mephibosheth to the palace. Mephibosheth was a bit shy at first. He might have been afraid of King David. But David invited him to eat with him. This was something very special.

David said to him, "I remember your father, Jonathan. He was my good friend. He helped me when I was in danger. Now I can help you. You may live

here with me and eat with me at my table. My servants will take care of the farm that used to be your father's. You don't have to worry about anything."

So Mephibosheth lived at the palace and was happy there. He was glad that David would take care of him. David was very kind to him.

2. Pray: "Thank-you, God, that David was kind to someone who needed him. Help me to be kind to people, too. Amen."

3. Sing songs (see pages 175-176). Include other favourites.

Group Activities

1. Play games. The children will "need" or "help" at least one other child.

I Need You puzzle. Two children try to match a two- or four-piece puzzle and put the puzzle together.

Teacher

- Have ready one picture (cut into two or four distinctive pieces) for every two children; divide the pieces in half and put in separate envelopes.
- Hand each child an envelope containing half of a puzzle.
- Tell the children they need to find someone whom they can help.

Children

- Find someone who has puzzle pieces similar to yours and put your puzzle together.

Relays. Most simple relays will work here. Choose ones that involve an object that needs to be shared like running with a ball or hitting a balloon. Emphasize "helping" each other by bringing the object to them to use, having fun rather than "winning."

I'm Hungry relay. Have a teacher or leader for each group of children. The teacher calls out, "I'm hungry, please feed me." Children take turns bringing items from their bowl that could feed the teacher (Ping-Pong ball on a spoon for an egg, an apron to wear, paper plate carried on your head, cup with water, egg beater, apple, etc.). Have one item for each child in the group. Teacher should hold or wear each item that is brought to add to the humour.

Please Help Me relay. The teacher starts with a very simple story about something breaking and needing to be fixed. Each child in the group runs to the hammer and peg set (or other such set of tools) and pounds one peg into board until all are done and the item is "fixed."

2. Work together. Make and serve cookies. Using a sugar cookie recipe and heart-shaped cutouts, let the children bake and/or decorate cookies. Invite some guests to be served by the children (a pastor, church secretary, parents, the custodian). The children could set the table complete with their centrepieces. The children will want to join their guests, so make enough cookies for them as well.

3. Share a snack. If you made cookies together, have them for your snack. A special treat such as ice-cream bars might illustrate that loving God and loving others belong together—you can't have one without the other.

4. Retell the story. Encourage the children to act out the story. They can take turns being the different characters: David, Ziba, Mephibosheth.

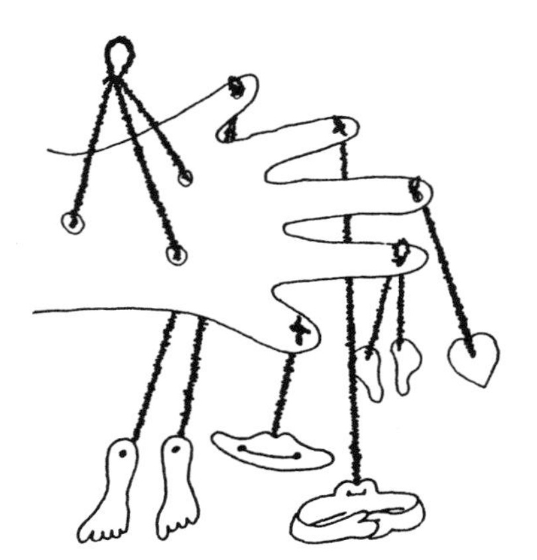

5. Memorize the Bible verse: Share what you have and be generous (1 Timothy 6:18, paraphrased).

Centres

1. Mobile. Add feet for the symbol (see illustration).

Teacher
- Out of fun foam, precut two feet shapes per child.
- Punch hole in heel of each foot.
- Have ready two chenille stems and three beads per child.

Children
- Attach one end of both chenille stems to the last finger on the hand.
- Secure with a bead.
- Attach the other end of chenille stems to each foot, securing with beads.

2. Take-home craft. Make table centrepieces. Use the theme of being kind to those in need, and relate the centrepiece to hosting guests. This centrepiece can be used at home when the child's family is hosting guests. Send a note home requesting parental guidance in lighting the candles.

Teacher
- Precut scraps of material in squares (5 cm., 2 in.) with pinking shears. About 20-40 pieces are needed per child.
- Precut Styrofoam balls (5 or 6 cm., 2 or 2 1/2 in.) in half. Each child needs one-half of a ball.

Children
- Place a scrap of material on the Styrofoam ball. With a pointed object (i.e, nut pick or plastic bobby pin), push the scrap into the ball. Leave space at the top to insert a small candle. Cover the rest of the ball.

Teacher
- Insert a small candle into the centre of the Styrofoam.

3. Special activities. Make Personalized Sandals. When we help others, we are active and use our feet. Make sandals for the children's feet as reminders.

Teacher
- Precut oval shapes (30 x 13 cm., 8 x 5 in.) from corrugated cardboard, two per child.
- Punch six holes in each as shown on the pattern, page 166.
- Have ready gimp or cord elastic pieces (1-m., 1-yd.), two per child.

Children
- Put one foot on each cardboard piece with toes at the end even with the two centre holes.
- Have someone trace around each foot with a crayon. (Do not cut the foot shape out.)
- Starting on the top side of the heel end of the cardboard, "sew" elastic down and up, continuing to top toe holes. Loop elastic around the other elastic, tying the two pieces together. Continue through all the holes; end at heel.

Teacher
- Knot the ends of gimp or elastic together, adjusting to fit. Leave 15-20 centimeters, 6-8 inches, at the ends for tying a bow.

Children
- To wear the sandals, slide feet under all elastic loops, so that the elastic loops come up next to the big toe and the knot rests in front of the ankle.

4. Books/tapes. Choose from the following or other appropriate titles:

- *Frog and Toad All Year*, Arnold Lobel (HarperCollins, 1976). The story "The Surprise" is applicable.
- *Cleversticks*, Bernard Ashley, illustrated by Derek Brazell (HarperCollins, 1992).
- *Wilfrid Gordon McDonald Partridge*, Mem Fox, illustrated by Julie Vivas (Penguin Books, 1984).

5. Toys. See page 132.

6. Colouring. See page 132.

Closing

Follow your closing ritual.

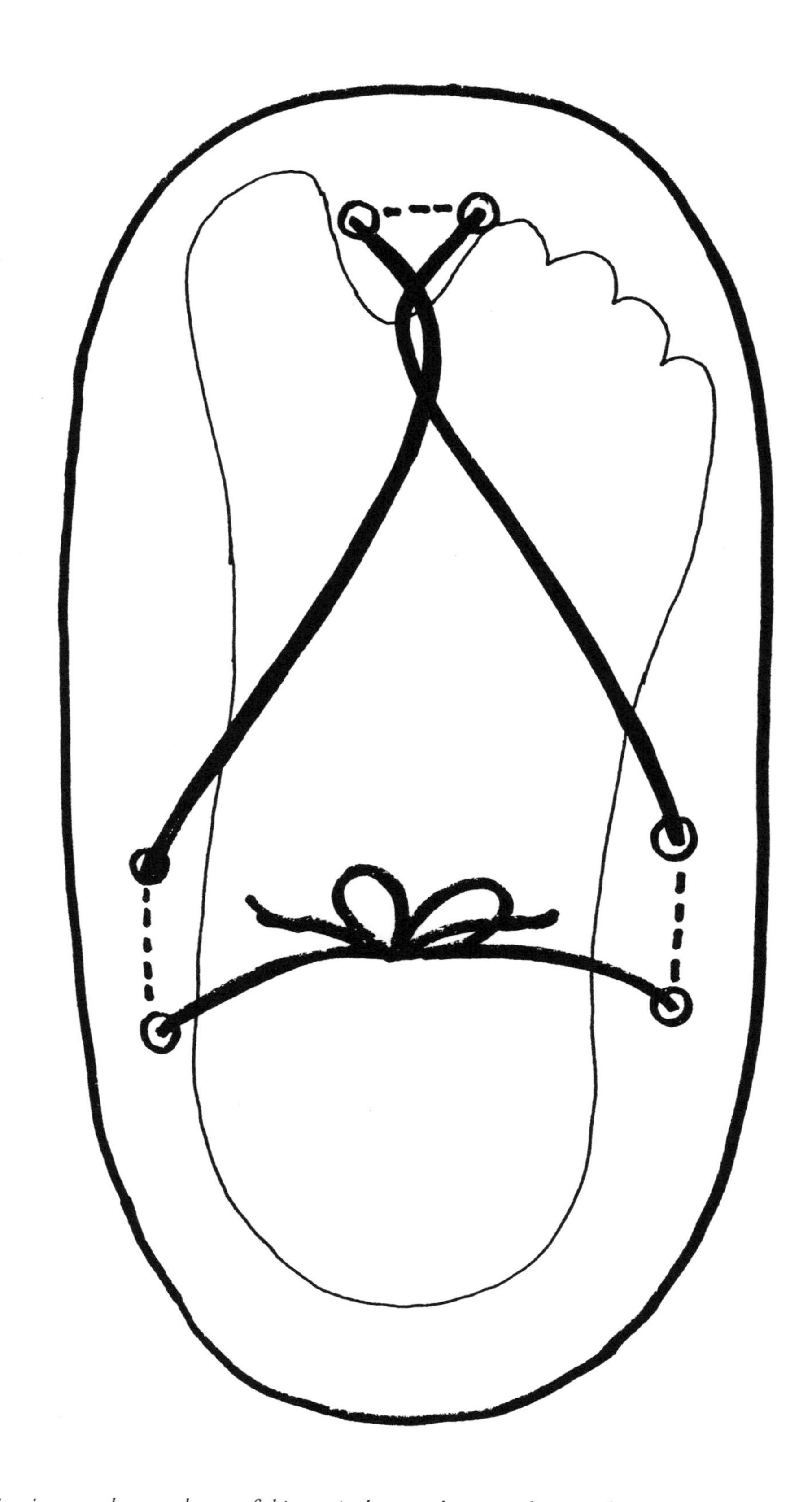

Permission is granted to purchasers of this curriculum to photocopy this page for use with the Loving God *curriculum.*

Resources

See pages 30-31 for a listing of resources for kindergarten through grade 5.

Books

Session 1

Murphy, Elspeth Campbell. *What Can I Say to You, God?* David and I Talk to God Series. (Elgin, Ill.: Chariot Books, David C. Cook, 1980).

Murphy, Elspeth Campbell. *Everybody, Shout Hallelujah!* David and I Talk to God Series. (Elgin, Ill.: Chariot Books, David C. Cook, 1980).

Caswell, Helen. *I Can Talk with God.* (Nashville, Tenn.: Abingdon Press, 1990).

Session 2

Cynthia. *The Night There Was Thunder and Stuff.* (Winfield, B.C.: Wood Lake Books, 1993).

Murphy, Elspeth Campbell. *I'm Listening, God*, David and I Talk to God Series. (Elgin, Ill.: Chariot Books, David C. Cook, 1983).

Session 3

Lobel, Arnold. *Frog and Toad Are Friends.* (New York, N.Y.: HarperCollins Children's Books, 1970). The story entitled "The Letter" is appropriate.

Lobel, Arnold. *Days with Frog and Toad.* (New York, N.Y.: HarperCollins Children's Books, 1979). The story "Alone" is appropriate for the theme.

Foon, Dennis. *The Short Tree and the Bird That Could Not Sing.* (Toronto, Ont.: Groundwood-Douglas and McIntyre, 1991). This is a story of a special friendship.

Kasza, Keiko. *The Rat and the Tiger.* (New York, N.Y.: Putnam Publishing Group, 1993).

Derby, Janice. *Are You My Friend?* (Scottdale, Penn.: Herald Press, 1993).

Session 4

Lobel, Arnold. *Days with Frog and Toad.* (New York, N.Y.: HarperCollins Children's Books, 1979). The stories "The Kite" and "The Hat" fit into this theme.

Crary, Elizabeth. *Children's Problem Solving Series.* (Parenting Press). These books help to raise children's awareness of ways to resolve social conflict:

I Can't Wait (How can Luke get a turn on the trampoline?).

I Want to Play (How can Danny find someone to play with?).

My Name Is Not Dummy (How can Jenny get Eduardo to stop calling her a dummy?).

I Want It (What can Amy do when Megan has the truck she wants?).

Lehn, Cornelia. *The Sun and the Wind.* (Scottdale, Penn.: Herald Press, 1987).

Bartolonew. *Jimmy and the White Lie.* (St. Louis, Mo.: Concordia Publishing House, 1976).

Session 5

Lobel, Arnold. *Frog and Toad All Year.* (New York, N.Y.: HarperCollins Children's Books, 1976). The story "The Surprise" is applicable.

Ashley, Bernard. *Cleversticks.* (New York, N.Y.: Crown Books, 1992).

Fox, Mem. *Wilfrid Gordon McDonald Partridge.* (Brooklyn, N.Y.: Kane Miller Books, 1985).

Murphy, Elspeth Campbell. *What Can I Say to You, God?* David and I Talk to God Series. (Elgin, Ill., Chariot Books, David C. Cook, 1980).

Joni's Kids Activity Book. "Different But Friends," by Joy MacKenzie with Joni Eareckson Tada (Word Music, 1985).

Puppet plays

HANNAH
Session 1

Loving God by Praying

Puppets: three sheep named Curly, Muffy, and Buffy (one identifying characteristic per sheep; e.g., colour, hat)
Dog
Shepherd
Props: one large tree on the side of the stage

[*Play begins as two of the sheep are playing hide-and-seek together and Curly is watching from behind the tree.*]

Curly: Silly sheep, playing silly baby games! Well, I don't care. I don't need them. I can play by myself.
Dog: [*Comes onstage, beside Curly.*] Hi, Curly! What can you play by yourself?
Curly: Hide-and-seek, that's what.
Dog: Ha, ha! Oh, Curly, that game takes two to play! There has to be someone to hide and someone to find you. You can't hide from yourself! Ha, ha!
Curly: Well, maybe not that game, but I can play another one! I don't need anyone to play with! [*Goes offstage, angrily. Muffy and Buffy, who were playing together, now stop and come to Dog.*]
Muffy: Hi, Dog! What's wrong with Curly?
Dog: I think he feels left out. You were playing hide-and-seek without him. Why didn't you let him play with you?
Buffy: Well, because he always says we play baby games.
Muffy: Yeah, and he never plays fair!
Buffy: Yeah, and he gets angry and won't take his turn at being It.
Dog: That's too bad! I wish Curly would learn to cooperate with others or he will always feel left out. [*Dog and Muffy and Buffy go offstage.*]
Curly: [*Comes onstage.*] I don't need them! I can play by myself! [*Curly runs back and forth across stage several times.*] Oh, dear! This isn't very much fun!
Shepherd: Hello, Curly! What were you doing?
Curly: I was chasing myself, but it wasn't any fun.
Shepherd: Why were you chasing yourself?
Curly: Because I don't have any friends to play with! The other sheep don't want to play with me.
Shepherd: If you want to have friends, you must learn to be one.
Curly: How can I be a friend?
Shepherd: You could ask God to help you.
Curly: [*Prays.*] Dear God, please help me to be friendly to others. Teach me what I can do to be a friend, and help me to have friends.
Shepherd: [*Hugs Curly.*] Now Curly, I know God hears us when we pray, so let's go find the other sheep and let God help you make friends. [*Shepherd and Curly go offstage together.*]

By Elizabeth R. Eby

Permission is granted to purchasers of this curriculum to photocopy this page for use with the Loving God *curriculum.*

Loving God by Listening

Puppets: Curly, Muffy, Buffy, Dog, Shepherd
Props: one large tree on the side of the stage

[*Play begins with all sheep and the Shepherd onstage.*]

Shepherd: My dear little sheep, today I want you to stay on this side of the tree. I heard a bear this morning nearby, so don't wander off.

Muffy: We must listen to what the Shepherd says. I think he knows what is best for us.

Buffy: Yeah, and we can still eat and play here on this side of the tree.

Muffy: Come on, Curly! Let's play hide-and-seek together now. You can hide first, Curly. I'll be It. [*Muffy and Buffy go offstage.*]

Curly: Hm-m-m. I wonder where I should hide. I'm so glad I can play with Muffy and Buffy today. Hey, I know a place where they won't look for me. [*Curly hides on the other side of the tree. Muffy and Buffy come up onstage, looking everywhere for Curly.*]

Muffy/Buffy: Curly! Curly!

[*Offstage, the sound of a growling bear is heard. Muffy and Buffy begin to shake in fear.*]

Muffy: Oh dear! Where is Curly?

Buffy: Maybe the bear has found him! Let's run and tell Dog!

Muffy: Dog! Dog! [*Muffy runs to the opposite side of the tree, calling for Dog. Up comes Dog.*] Oh, Dog! There you are! Please hurry and help Curly! We think the bear has found him!

[*Muffy and Buffy go offstage. Dog looks everywhere and finally looks on the other side of the tree.*]

Dog: Oh Curly! I thought the Shepherd told you not to go on the other side of the tree. Please come home at once! [*Dog barks and grabs at Curly, and pushes him gently to the other side of the tree and into the middle of the stage.*]

Curly: [*Pouting.*] Last time I play with anyone! [*Dog goes away to get Shepherd.*]

Shepherd: [*Comes onstage beside Curly.*] Oh Curly! The other sheep told me they thought the bear found you, and then Dog told me that you did not listen to me and hid on the other side of the tree! I'm so glad you're all right! Why did you not stay where I asked you to?

Curly: Well, I did not really want to listen to you because it was such a good hiding place.

Shepherd: Oh Curly! I knew there was a bear somewhere out there beyond the tree and that is why I told you not to go there. I wanted you to listen to me, because I care very much about you, Curly.

Curly: Oh, I love you, too! You are my Shepherd!

Shepherd: When you love someone, Curly, you will want to listen and obey them. The other sheep were worried about you. Did you hear them calling you?

Curly: No, I didn't. I guess I wasn't listening.

Shepherd: God is our Good Shepherd, Curly, and loves us very much. God wants us to listen carefully to God's voice, because God knows what is best for us, too. [*Shepherd hugs Curly, and both go offstage.*]

Permission is granted to purchasers of this curriculum to photocopy this page for use with the Loving God *curriculum.*

Session 3
JONATHAN

Loving God by Loving Others

Puppets: Curly, Muffy, Buffy, Dog, Shepherd, and a bear
Props: one large tree on the side of the stage

[*Play begins with dog and all sheep onstage.*]

Dog: The Shepherd heard the bear growling this morning somewhere out there beyond that tree. So stay together and eat and play quietly. Be sure not to go to the other side of the tree. [*Dog goes offstage.*]

Muffy: Oooh! I'm scared! Let's stay together.

Buffy: Yeah, I'm afraid too. And I'm hungry. Let's eat some of this grass.

Curly: [*Starts to eat.*] Aw, this grass is okay, but I bet the grass on the other side of the tree is even better.

Muffy: Well, it may be, but we must obey Dog and Shepherd. We have to stay here.

Curly: Well, I know that I should obey, but that grass beyond the tree does look so much more tasty. I think I will try it.

Buffy: Oh, no, Curly! Don't go! [*Muffy and Buffy huddle close together on one side of the stage while Curly goes to the other side of the stage, just past the tree. Behind Curly a bear pops up on stage. Curly does not seem to see him at first.*]

Bear: Oh, look! A tasty lamb for my breakfast! GRRRRRR!

Curly: [*Turns and sees Bear.*] Oh! Oh! Help me! Help me! [*Bear chases Curly around the tree.*]

Muffy: Oh no! That bear is chasing Curly. We must help Curly!

Buffy: But how can we help? I'm scared, too!

Muffy: We must help Curly to get away. We can let the bear chase us instead! [*Muffy and Buffy run towards the bear.*]

Bear: [*Stops chasing Curly.*] Oh look! Two lambs for breakfast! I'm so hungry! [*Bear begins to chase Muffy and Buffy while Curly slips away offstage.*]

Curly: [*Shouting.*] I will get help! [*Dog comes onstage, barking and growling and chases Bear away. Curly comes back onstage with the Shepherd.*]

Shepherd: Oh, my dear little sheep! Are you all right?

Buffy: Yes, Shepherd! Dog is chasing the bear away now.

Shepherd: Curly told me what you did to try to save him from the bear. You sure were very brave to help him.

Muffy: Well, Curly is our friend and we love him.

Shepherd: Then you must love God, too. God asks us to show how much we love God by showing love to others.

Curly: Thank-you all for loving me and being my friends. [*All hug.*]

Permission is granted to purchasers of this curriculum to photocopy this page for use with the Loving God *curriculum.*

Loving God by Making Peace

Puppets: Muffy, Buffy, Curly, Dog, and Shepherd
Props: one large tree on the side of the stage and a brightly coloured flower in the middle of the stage

[*Play begins as all the sheep come onstage, laughing and playing.*]
Muffy: Oh, look! What a pretty flower!
Buffy: It must have grown here overnight.
Muffy: [*Smells flower.*] Hm-m-m. It sure does smell good!
Curly: [*Bends over flower.*] I bet it tastes good, too!
Buffy: Oh no! Don't eat it! It is too beautiful.
Muffy/Buffy: We want to smell the flower some more.
Curly: Get out of the way! I want to smell it, too! [*The sheep begin to fight, pushing and shoving at each other. Then all the sheep try to grab the flower at the same time.*]
Buffy/Muffy: Let us have it!
Curly: No! I want it! [*There is more arguing, until finally the flower becomes broken at the stem, and the sheep are now tugging at the flower.*]
Dog: [*Comes onstage.*] STOP IT! STOP IT! What is going on here? [*Dog barks and snatches the flower away from the sheep. Dog runs offstage with the flower.*]
Shepherd: [*Comes onstage.*] My little sheep, why are you fighting?
Muffy/Buffy: It was our flower!
Curly: No, I saw it first. It was my flower!
Muffy: You did not see it first! I did!
Curly: Did not!
Muffy: Did too! [*Buffy comes to stand between Muffy and Curly.*]
Buffy: Please stop fighting. It does not matter who saw the flower first. The flower is not even here anymore, so why are we still fighting?! [*Muffy and Curly stand quietly looking at each other, and then they start laughing.*]
Curly: You are right! We are arguing over nothing.
Shepherd: Thank-you, Buffy! You really helped Curly and Muffy to solve their problem. God really wants us to be able to play peacefully with each other.
Muffy: I still think that the flower was so pretty. I am sad that we can no longer enjoy it.
Buffy: Let's go and find Dog. Maybe we could ask him to bring the flower to the sheepfold. We could put it into water, and then we can all enjoy its beauty for a long time.
All: Oh, yes! [*All exit happily.*]

Permission is granted to purchasers of this curriculum to photocopy this page for use with the Loving God *curriculum.*

Session 5
DAVID

Loving God by Showing Kindness

Puppets: Muffy, Buffy, Curly, Dog, Shepherd
Props: one large tree on the side of the stage
basket full of grass
large bone
one piece of fruit (apple, orange, etc.)

[*Play begins as all sheep come onstage, walking slowly, apparently very sad.*]
Curly: Come on, guys! Let's get something to eat.
Muffy: No, I am not very hungry.
Curly: Well, then let's play hide-and-seek.
Buffy: No, I don't really feel like playing today. [*Dog comes onstage.*]
Dog: Hi, sheep! You all look pretty sad today! What's wrong?
Muffy: Do you remember that flower we were fighting about the other day? You know, you helped us bring it back to the sheep-fold.
Dog: Yes, I remember.
Buffy: [*Sadly.*] Well, it has withered and dried up and now it is no longer beautiful to look at.
Curly: And it no longer smells sweet, either!
Dog: Aw, I'm sorry, little sheep. But I must go now. I will be back in a little while to take you to the Shepherd. [*Muffy and Buffy go slowly to the side of the stage, while Curly goes near the tree.*]
Curly: I am sorry that my friends feel so sad today. I wish I could cheer them up somehow. They have been so kind to me. Even when I disobeyed, they still remained my friends. I sure wish I could help them. Hey wait! I have an idea! [*Curly runs off-stage past the tree.*]
Muffy: Come on, Buffy. We better eat something here before we have to go back home.
Buffy: Yea, I guess. But this grass isn't very tasty. [*Curly comes onstage, carrying a basket full of green grass.*]
Curly: Hey, guys! Look! I have a surprise for you! [*Muffy and Buffy run towards Curly.*]
Muffy/Buffy: What is the surprise? What do you have? [*Curly shows them the basket of grass.*]
Muffy/Buffy: Oh, fresh green grass! Where did you get this?
Curly: Well, from the other side of the tree.
Muffy/Buffy: Curly!
Curly: I didn't go far beyond the tree, and Shepherd was with me. I thought you both might like to share this fresh grass.
Muffy: Oh, thank-you, Curly! It looks so good!
Buffy: Yeah, thanks, Curly, for being so kind! [*While sheep are eating, Dog comes up onstage.*]
Dog: Hm-m-m. You have a nice treat today! That makes me hungry, too!
[*Curly slips away and comes back onstage carrying a large bone.*]
Curly: Here, Dog. I found this one day. It is for you.
Dog: For me? Oh, Curly! It does look delicious. Thank-you! [*Begins*

Permission is granted to purchasers of this curriculum to photocopy this page for use with the Loving God *curriculum.*

gnawing on bone, then stops.] Come now, sheep. We must get back to the sheepfold, but we can take our treats with us. [*Dog, Muffy, and Buffy begin to leave the stage.*]

Dog: Come on, Curly. It is time to go.

Curly: May I stay here and wait for the Shepherd?

Dog: Well, I guess that would be all right. [*Dog, Muffy, and Buffy all leave stage. Shepherd comes onstage.*]

Shepherd: Oh, Curly! Here you are! It is time to go back to the sheepfold now.

Curly: In a minute! [*Curly disappears offstage, and reappears quickly with a piece of fruit.*] This is for you, Shepherd!

Shepherd: What? Why, thank-you Curly! You are very kind.

Curly: You have all been so good to me. I wanted to do something special for you.

Shepherd: Well, you have certainly made me happy by sharing a really good gift with me. God wants us to be helpful and kind. I love you, Curly.

Curly: And I love you, too.

Shepherd: And God loves us all. [*Shepherd and Curly hug.*]

Permission is granted to purchasers of this curriculum to photocopy this page for use with the Loving God *curriculum.*

Songs

Love, Love (theme song)

One, Two, Three

Copyright © 1977 by Evangel Press, Nappanee, Ind. 46550; Faith & Life Press, Newton, Kans. 67114; Mennonite Publishing House, Scottdale, Penn. 15683. Reprinted from *Sing with Me* by permission.

I'm Gonna Pray (see Worship, page 58)

Make Peace (see Worship, page 59)

Junior Youth

Introduction

The Junior Youth section contains complete session plans for grades 6 through 8, ages eleven through thirteen (completed grades 6-8).

Organization

The junior youth will be part of the larger worship assembly that includes children in the kindergarten to grade 5 programme. They also may choose to join the larger group for the Closing.

While the children in the kindergarten to grade 5 programme participate in their three-way rotation of Talk and Move, Pray and Listen, and Make and Take, the junior youth will have their own 105-minute session.

The junior youth will form a separate small group for the Gather and Greet. This is a time to take attendance, do group-building activities, introduce the theme of the day, and collect the offering.

Leadership

It would be helpful if you are familiar with the main body of the curriculum. Check with the *Loving God* coordinator for more information about the general outline and format, for the memory texts, music and worship dramas, and responsibilities of the Group leaders.

The leaders for the junior youth are adults who love God and enjoy this age-group. The leaders should encourage the natural and spiritual development of the youth and value them as they begin to search for an identity as young adults. Being an active listener and a facilitator who can be invitational in discussion and activity times are important characteristics of junior youth leaders.

Be an advocate for these young people, intent on helping them grow into a loving relationship with God. Model your love for God. Encourage the group leaders to do the same.

Characteristics of junior youth

Junior youth are moving into adolescence, a time of great change in their emotions and attitudes. A positive self-esteem is very important for this age-group. Junior youth tend to worry about their looks, actions, feelings, acceptance by peers, parents, and other significant adults. In this time together, help them to feel accepted, comfortable, and positive about themselves.

Some junior youth are beginning to think about faith issues in a new way. As their skills in abstract conceptualization mature, they are able to question and reflect upon the Bible stories and God's activity in the world. They can begin to develop a more personal relationship with God and explore appropriate ways of responding to God.

Junior youth are in that exciting stage of life between childhood and youth. As they mature toward adolescence and independence, they need adult models who can help them make the transition as smoothly as possible. Separating the junior youth into their own group gives them time and permission to explore faith and life issues at an age-appropriate level. As they work together in their own group, they will feel special and unique.

Special items

Service project

You may want to make plans for one or two service projects that you feel may enrich the experiences of the students, and which will help them to put into practice what they are learning about loving and responding to God. The themes for Sessions 3, 4, and 5 especially lend themselves to this type of practical involvement. Perhaps there is a food bank in your community that would welcome help in sorting donations, or a nursing home that would welcome visitors, or a church-sponsored local agency such as a soup kitchen or a Mennonite Central Committee SELFHELP organization that could use some willing volunteers. Try to identify what some of the needs in your local community or church might be, and make arrangements to have the junior youth become involved.

If you choose to leave the property, consider the time factor and ask for written parental permission. You may wish to check insurance policies for transporting children, etc. Take into consideration the needs and size of the group.

Consider making an appropriate item that could be shared with the people they will be visiting or helping. Incorporate the gift item into your craft project during the sessions that precede your visit.

Memory texts

The Bible memory texts for the week are found on page 105. Text from both the New International Version and the New Revised Standard Version are given. Or choose another appropriate version that fits your group. Encourage the students to discuss the meaning of the texts and invite them to work with the texts in various ways, such as writing their own litany, putting it to music, or expressing the meaning of the verses in their own words. Other ideas for encouraging memorization can be found on pages 105-109. Be a co-learner with the students, and memorize the texts yourself!

Craft suggestions

For the Response section of each session, choose a craft that will be ongoing for the week or several days. On most days, there is a suggestion for a craft that can be completed in one session. Take into account your own preferences and level of comfort with any of the suggestions. Try to determine which of the suggestions would be most suitable for your specific group.

Felt Door Hanging

Use the directions found in the kindergarten through grade 5 Make and Take Resource, pages 113-114, for making a felt door hanging. If desired, arrangements could be made with the Make and Take leader to work with the Junior Youth as a group to make this particular craft. Junior Youth would be able to express themselves through the medium of fabric, and they would be able to work at their own level. Some of the symbols for the door hanging could be adapted to be used on posters or separate wall hangings for a specific session's project. Separate posters would work especially well for Sessions 1, 3, and 4.

Wooden Plaque

Use the logo "Loving God," page 29, to make a wooden plaque. Using wood-burning techniques, the logo could be engraved onto a decorative piece of wood. Employ your own skills in this area, or locate someone in the congregation who might enjoy sharing his or her expertise with the junior youth. This project may take several days.

Banner

As a gift to the church, plan to make a series of banners that illustrate the Scripture texts for the week. The students could work together in groups to make this gift. Use felt with cutout letters, incorporating the logo, to create a series of banners (see illustration, p. 181). You may wish to contact someone in your congregation who could advise you on colours, size, and design that would be suitable for your facilities.

Quilt

Symbolize the concepts of the week by making a quilt consisting of various squares of material decorated with an appropriate symbol from the session's learning. Fabric crayons or bubble paints could be used. Each person could contribute a square to the quilt each day. At the end of the week, sew the squares together to make a wall hanging. If there is skill and interest, the quilt could be filled, bound, and knotted. Enlist the help of senior adults in your congregation.

Additional Crafts

There are always some students who finish their work ahead of the others. Have available several meaningful activities with which students can challenge themselves. Books relating to the theme of loving God, of prayer, and stories that tell of modern-day peacemakers could be set out in a book corner. Invite written responses and thoughts about the themes of the day by having a journal (blank book) available for additions during the week.

Love the
Lord your
God

with all
your
heart

with all
your
soul

with all
your
strength

and with
all your
mind

and your
neighbor
as yourself

Session plan

Pages 178-204 contain complete session plans and suggestions for teaching junior youth.

The suggestions given are to be used as guidelines for the creative teacher of junior youth. As leader, you know the needs and interests of the youth. Feel free to change and adapt the material as long as you keep in mind the focus and theme for the week. Study the biblical background and text for each day, reflecting on what you can learn from each of the characters from the book of Samuel.

Look over the entire Junior Youth Resource section and decide which crafts or response activities you are going to do with your group. Gather supplies and plan ahead of time so you have the supplies available when you need them.

Programme

Use the times for the separate sessions as guidelines. Be flexible in the timing. Consider the maturity and the size of the group when you plan the field trips or service projects. Do not, however, sacrifice the Bible study time. It is the Bible study that sets the agenda for the response activity. The Bible study and corresponding response will have a long-lasting impact on the lives of the junior youth.

Get Ready

Items needed and early preparation for the activities are listed. If *Loving God* is planned for a five-day programme, be sure you have checked supplies and ordered or collected necessary items well in advance for all the sessions.

Gather and Greet (15 minutes)

Junior youth will meet as a separate group for the opening time. Help the group choose a name that fits with the names chosen by the kindergarten through grade 5 groups. Meet in a classroom or out-of-doors. For every eight or ten junior youth, have an additional Group leader to assist you in discussions and the various response activities.

Use this time for group building, introductions, offering, and preparation for worship. Give out the name tags each day and collect them at the end of each session.

Worship (30 minutes)

Junior youth will join the kindergarten through grade 5 for worship. If you and the group enjoy drama, check with the drama coordinator to see how you might use their talents to help present the Bible stories.

Study and Discuss (45 minutes)

Review the Bible story, interpret the story at a junior youth level, and apply the truths learned to daily living. Provide Bibles for each youth so they can read the text each day. If possible, use a Bible translation that is easy for youth to read, such as *The Good News Bible.*

Each session, discuss the events of the biblical story and reflect on how this relates to the experiences of the junior youth. Establish an atmosphere of openness so that the youth are invited to explore their questions with you. Listen and learn from them as you appropriately share your own faith experiences with them.

Reflect and Remember

Prayer and reflection time are included so that the students can spend some time reflecting on what they've heard and are learning to grow in communication with God.

Take a Break (15 minutes)

Have a snack, relax, and/or play some active games. Check the games in the Talk and Move Resource, pages 61-82. These games have been chosen to correlate to the theme of the session. Your group may have a favourite game that they would enjoy playing as a break. If your group seems to manage unscheduled time well, allow them this time to chat, or just relax.

Respond (45 minutes)

A variety of response activities are suggested for several reasons. Junior youth have different learning preferences that need to be accommodated if you wish to hold their interest and attention. Some youth prefer to respond to the input through hands-on activities such as crafts or games. Others learn best by thinking, writing, or drawing. Still others want to be involved in some sort of active service project.

What you choose to do, then, will depend upon your interests as a leader, upon the availability of service agencies or persons to visit or help, and the interests of the junior youth. Plan to take at least one field trip. This will provide variety for the junior youth and help them to put into practice the concept of loving God by loving others, making peace, and showing kindness.

Refer to the Printed and Audiovisual Resources in Get it Organized, pages 30-31, for appropriate stories and resources that could be incorporated into your program.

Gather and Bless (15 minutes)

You have two options for this final assembly. You may choose to join the kindergarten through grade 5 group for singing and the closing blessing, or you may stay as a group for your own closing. If you choose to remain by yourselves, use this time to learn the blessing, "Go in Peace," page 30, and to review the memory texts, page 105.

Session plans for Junior Youth

Session 1

Hannah

Theme: Loving God by praying
Bible Text: 1 Samuel 1:1—2:1-11
Story Focus: Hannah demonstrated her love for God in her prayer life. She trusted that God would answer her prayer. She fulfilled her promise to God when she took Samuel to the temple to live with Eli.
Faith Focus: We show we love God when we talk to God. We trust that God will hear and answer us when we pray.

Get Ready

1. Gather "obstacles"—tires, pillows, chairs, boxes, boards, etc.—for Study and Discuss #3.
2. Make copies of Reflection Page so that each student will have one.
3. Prepare the Circle Session Cards, page 188, for Reflect and Remember #2. Cut the cards apart.

Gather and Greet (15 minutes)

Greet the students. Do necessary tasks, such as recording attendance, receiving offering, and, most importantly, establishing a welcoming environment.

Distribute name tags to the youth as they arrive. Invite them to put their own names on the prepared tag and decorate it if desired. Choose a name that is consistent with the other groups; e.g., a specific colour or name of a biblical character.

Do a group-building activity. Check page 186 for some suggestions as to how to facilitate positive group interaction. Use other exercises and activities that your group would find enjoyable and would help each one to feel accepted and welcome.

Worship

See page 178. Go with the junior youth to the assembly area for Worship. Stay with the group and model active participation during this time. Do any necessary preparations if the students will be involved in the drama.

Study and Discuss (45 minutes)

1. Play *Go to the Wall,* a true-false activity designed to help the students think about their own attitudes and opinions about prayer. How do we pray? What are appropriate things to pray about? What prevents us from praying? Why does it appear that God answers some prayers and not others? Then, there will be opportunity to read the biblical text and discuss their responses in a creative way.

Ask the students to stand and be prepared to "go to the wall" to indicate their response to the following true-false statements. Identify one wall or spot as "TRUE" and the opposite wall as "FALSE." Read each statement and have the students move to one wall or the other. Encourage them to make their decision without discussion or watching anyone else. Reassure them that there is no right or wrong answer.

What about prayer?

a. There is a right or wrong way to pray.
b. I pray only when I'm in trouble.
c. God always answers prayer.
d. God sometimes says "No" to our requests.
e. If I don't get what I request, there is something wrong with my faith.

2. Use your Bibles. Distribute a Bible to each person. Turn to the text found in 1 Samuel 1:1—2:1-11.

Invite the children to look over this passage silently and to choose one character of the story whose words they would be willing to read aloud. The characters are Elkanah, Hannah, Eli, and the narrator. When all have read silently, read the entire story aloud, with students reading their chosen part in an expressive way. If more students are willing to read parts, have them share the reading of one character's part. If there are those who choose not to read aloud, have them follow along in their Bibles as the text is read by the others.

Discuss. Reread the questions from the *Go to the Wall* game and invite the students to tell how Hannah might have responded to each one. How did Hannah's actions show what she believed about prayer and about God?

3. Use Hannah's experience of overcoming obstacles to encourage the students to understand how to get rid of the obstacles that stand in the way of their relationship with God. Divide the students into groups of about four. Give each group an index card and a pen. Ask them to talk with each other, and appoint one member of the group to write down their ideas about what Hannah's obstacles were.

Bring all the groups together. Ask each group to share their ideas and make a cooperative list on the chalkboard or on chart paper.

Give each smaller group the following instructions:

a. Choose one of the obstacles from the list.
b. Go to a pile of "obstacles" (tires, pillows, chairs, boxes, boards, etc.) and pick one object from the pile that symbolizes Hannah's obstacle.

c. On the large index card, write the obstacle of Hannah that you chose from the list.

d. On the back of the card, write what needs to be done to overcome the obstacle.

Bring all the groups together to work on making an obstacle course either in the room or in a hallway or outdoors. When completed, they can take turns negotiating the obstacles.

Reflect and Remember

1. Have students seated around a table or comfortably on the floor. Distribute the Reflection Page, "What Do I Think about Prayer?" (page 189), to each youth. Ask them to respond individually on their own sheets. They will be invited to share their responses only if they wish to.

When they have had several minutes for this activity, have them stop, even if they are not finished, and join the group. Invite the group to come together for a Circle Session.

2. Sit in a circle and think together about this question: How Do We Talk to God? Invite the students to participate in this short role-play exercise that explores the different ways of communication with someone in a position of authority.

Use the five Circle Session Cards on page 188. Put them into a small basket.

The leader can play the role of "the principal" in the following way: She or he sits casually in a chair set apart from the others, perhaps reading a magazine or doing some other "busywork" at a desk. The students choose one card from the basket. Each person, in turn, then approaches "the principal" and follows the instructions on the card. The "principal" indicates only a nonverbal response. The "principal" can indicate some frustration in the situations where she or he is only being asked for something, or told about his or her virtues. When the student with Card #5 initiates a real conversation, the "principal" should respond naturally when the student pauses.

3. Continue in the Circle Session activity. This activity encourages active listening, acceptance of everyone, respect for others, and expression of thoughts and feelings. Outline the "rules" for circle session.

a. Each person will be allowed to speak.

b. Each person is free to say whatever she or he wishes.

c. No one is allowed to interrupt, argue, comment, dispute, etc.

d. The leader will invite each person, in turn, to comment, and will simply say "thank-you" when that person is finished.

e. People are allowed to "pass" if they have no comments to give.

4. Debrief. After the role play has been completed, encourage discussion of the following questions:

- How do you think the principal felt in each of those situations?
- How is this like prayer?
- How do we view God when we pray?
- What might our prayers be like if we realize that prayer is a way of responding to God's love?
- What are good ways that we can talk to God?

5. After the concept of prayer has been discussed in this way, invite the youth to enter into a time of quiet reflection and prayer by themselves. Tell

them how this time of reflection will work, so that they can feel comfortable with the process.

Each student should find a quiet place where they can be alone, either in the classroom or in the sanctuary, if appropriate. Play some soft music during their time of reflection. When the music is over, that is their signal to move back together in the classroom. (Allow up to five minutes maximum.)

Encourage each one to spend the time in quiet thought, imagining how we feel in the presence of a close friend. When we are with someone who loves us deeply, we can share our feelings, tell about our needs, talk about things that bother us, and be assured our friend understands.

Model a short prayer as you invite God to listen to the prayers of the children. (You could use the song "Lord, Listen to your Children Praying" found in the Worship Resources section, page 57, as an appropriate beginning to this time of reflection.)

Take a Break (15 min.)

1. Have a simple snack.
2. Allow the students to stretch and have a brief, unscheduled time.

Respond (45 min.)

See page 180 for ideas for an ongoing craft. If you prefer to do a craft or response activity that can be completed in this session, make yeast pretzels.

Explain the pretzel story as follows:

The pretzel is made in the shape of crossed arms. When pretzels were first made, they were called "little arms." Monks in Europe are believed to have made the first pretzels. Monks spent a long time praying each day. When they prayed, they would cross their arms over their chest as a sign of reverence. In order to help the children understand that praying every day was important, the monks gave the children a small reward for saying their prayers. The reward was a piece of bread dough shaped like the crossed arms of a child praying.

Soft Pretzels

Measure out four cups of flour.

Add 1 teaspoon salt and 1 tablespoon instant yeast.

Mix together, then add 1 1/2 cups of hot tap water.

Knead the dough until smooth. Cut into small pieces. Using your hands, roll the dough into ropes and twist into the pretzel shape.

Place on a lightly greased cookie sheet.

Whip 1 egg. Using a pastry brush, brush egg onto the dough.

Sprinkle with coarse salt and bake at 425 degrees for 12 to 15 minutes. Allow to cool.

Gather and Bless (15 min.)

Explain to the group what your closing ritual will be—going to the larger assembly area or staying with your own group. Encourage group members to invite their friends to join them for the rest of the sessions. Give any necessary instructions or handouts before you dismiss the group.

Circle Session Cards

#1

Approach the principal and say in a singsong-type voice:
"We think you're great,
You really rate,
Thanks for letting us
Participate."
Do a little curtsy or bow, and quickly leave.

#2

Approach the principal and say in a very serious manner:

"You are the greatest principal. You do so much work around our school. You know everything. Your leadership is marvelous. You are definitely the best principal in the world."

Then, turn around and leave promptly.

#3

Rush up to the principal and say in a loud voice:

"Please sir, come down to Room 8! There's been an accident! I think one of the students has slipped and maybe broken her leg! Please, we need your help right away!"

Turn around and rush away again.

#4

Approach the principal very hesitantly, kneel down, and say in a pleading voice:

"Oh, sir, I know you are very busy. I'm sure you don't have time for someone like me. But please, sir, even though I am only a lowly student, would you be able to get me some pens and paper for the classroom? I hope it's not too much to ask. If it's not convenient for you to do this, I'll understand."

Then steal quietly away.

#5

Approach the principal, pull up a chair, and sit down fairly close to him or her. In a conversational tone, say:

"Hello, there! How are you? (Pause) You know, I really appreciate all the work you do around the school. You have been so supportive to me. (Pause) There are a few things I'd like you to know about that are going on around here. Did you know our class won the basketball tournament? (Pause) And next week, we are going on a field trip to the Science Centre. I guess you've been there before. Would you be able to recommend an exhibit that we should be sure not to miss? (Pause) Great, then, I'll be on my way. It was good to talk to you. See you tomorrow!"

Wave in a friendly fashion and exit.

Reflection Page

What Do I Think about Prayer?

Name: ______________________________

Complete each sentence.

1. I learned to pray by

____

____

____

____

2. The times I usually pray are

____

____

____

____

3. I don't feel like praying when

____

____

____

____

4. I pray best when

____

____

____

____

5. I feel that God answered my prayer when

____

____

____

____

Permission is granted to purchasers of this curriculum to photocopy this page for use with the Loving God *curriculum.*

Session 2

Samuel

Theme: Loving God by Listening
Bible Text: 1 Samuel 2:18-21; 26; 3:1-21
Story Focus: When Samuel realized that God was calling to him, he responded by listening to God's voice.
Faith Focus: We show that we love God when we listen for God's voice and respond.

Get Ready

1. Have paper and pencils available for Reflect and Remember.
2. Write the questions for Study and Discuss #2 on the board or chart paper.
3. Plan ahead for Session 4, Respond.

Gather and Greet (15 min.)

Distribute name tags. Welcome newcomers to class with a personal greeting and introductions to the group.

Continue with group-building activities. Try the following exercise. Play a version of the game of *Telephone*. Have one person begin by whispering a message to the person next to him or her. Have one person (whom you ask beforehand) deliberately change the message to something completely different. When the last person receives the message, ask him or her to share it.

Discuss what happened and how the message changed. Let the group know that this was a setup! What do we need in order to understand each other? Talk about the latest tools of communication available to us today. How do they help or hinder our communication? Encourage the students to notice the types of communication that the characters in today's Bible story drama will be experiencing.

Go with the group to Worship. Encourage full participation of all junior youth in Worship.

Study and Discuss (45 min.)

Review the Bible story and reflect together on how we listen to God's voice. How do we learn to listen to God with our "inner ear"? How did Samuel experience God's voice?

1. Practice listening. Give each person an index card and a marker. Have them go outside on the pavement or on the grass. Give them three minutes in which to make a list of all the sounds they hear. Call time and gather the group back together.

Compile a list of all the sounds heard in this way: Give each person an equal number of jellybeans, pennies, or dried beans. The first person names the first thing on their list. The leader records that sound on the chart paper. If anyone else has recorded the same thing, the first person gives a jellybean to each one who has heard the same sound and recorded it on his or her card. If no one else has recorded that sound, they must each give him or her a jellybean. Continue around the circle in this manner until everyone has been able to share the sounds they heard.

2. Hand out Bibles and ask the youth to read the text silently. Ask them to think about the following questions: What was Samuel's problem with listening? What is one thing about this story that surprises you? What is one thing that was new to you about this story?

Invite the students to find a partner to work with. After they have read the text silently and thought about their own response, give them time to talk about the questions with their partner. Then discuss the questions as a group and invite them to share whatever questions they might have about this text.

Ask them to consider the following questions: How do we listen to God today? How are we able to be alert to God's voice? What are the different ways we hear God speak to us?

List their responses on the chalkboard or chart paper if this seems appropriate.

3. Do interviews. Provide the students with clipboards and pens and paper, tape recorders, or video cameras for interviews with various people. They could work individually or with partners. The purpose of the interview is to find out from others what experiences they have had in hearing the voice of God.

Interview one of the congregation's ministers. Ask how that person has experienced God speaking to him or her.

Be a roving reporter. Search out available adults anywhere throughout the building and ask them the question "What is the best way to listen to God?" Perhaps the early childhood group who are also learning about this theme could be interviewed. Record all the answers and meet back together to share the results of the interviews.

Reflect and Remember

1. Read the litany on page 91. The leader can read the verses, and the group can respond with the All response.

2. Invite the children to reflect quietly in one of the following ways:

a. Guide the children in prayer. Invite the children to find a comfortable spot by themselves, but within hearing distance of you. Relax and get comfortable in your space. Imagine that you are in a favourite spot where you can think quietly. It may be outside or inside. Listen to the sounds around you in your imaginary place. What do you hear that is relaxing and comforting? Imagine that God is beside you in your favourite spot. Welcome God to sit beside you. Tell God that you are ready to listen to what God wants to tell you. Sit quietly and wait. What might God say to you about you or your family or your friends?

b. Encourage individual reflection. Allow the children to experience their own time of quiet reflection while soft music is playing. Invite them to consider what God might be saying to them. We can imagine that God is with us any time and any place. God is everywhere. What an awesome God! Encourage those who wish to write during this time to do so. Putting thoughts on paper in the form of a poem or prayer is an effective style of communication for some people.

Take a Break (15 min.)

1. Serve a snack.
2. Play an active game or provide some unscheduled break time.

Respond (45 min.)

Choose as many of these activities as time allows.

1. Continue with the ongoing craft activities begun during Session 1.

2. Spend time planning for a service project for Session 3. See page 179 for service project ideas. Or make arrangements to visit a local nursing home with the purpose of listening to and interacting with the elderly people there. As leader, assume the major responsibilities for the details and arrangements, but allow the youth as much input and opportunity to organize as possible. Several different groups could work on organizing the following areas.

a. Prepare appropriate questions to ask in an "interview" format. Find out what life was like for this person—daily chores, transportation methods, wages, family life, trips taken, most memorable experiences. As the leader, be certain that the people the youth visit are open to this type of interview and would enjoy it.

b. Plan and organize several games that could be played with the seniors and youth, such as bingo or card games.

c. Prepare an appropriate token gift to be shared with the residents. See craft ideas on page 180.

d. Prepare a snack food item, such as Rice Krispies squares or friendship cookies. Use a sugar cookie recipe to make heart-shaped cookies and decorate them.

Gather and Bless (15 min.)

Conduct your closing rituals. Give each person a parting blessing and enthusiastically look forward to their return tomorrow!

Session 3

Jonathan

Theme: Loving God by Loving Others
Bible Text: 1 Samuel 20:1-42
Biblical Background: 1 Samuel 18 and 19
Story Focus: Jonathan risked his life for his best friend, David, though it meant danger for him.
Faith Focus: We show we love God when we are a true friend.

Get Ready

1. Prepare the sample interview questions for Study and Discuss #2, page 195.
2. Have construction-paper heart shapes available for Study and Discuss #3, page 194.

Gather and Greet (15 min.)

Greet each person individually. Welcome any newcomers. Distribute name tags. Do necessary housekeeping items.

Ask the youth to think about important qualities of a best friend. What kinds of things do friends do for each other? Have them look for qualities of friendship they see demonstrated during Worship.

Worship

Go as a group to Worship and listen expectantly to the Bible story drama. Sing and pray as you praise God together.

Study and Discuss (45 min.)

Consider the qualities of a good friendship. What does it mean to take a risk for a friend? How is God's love like that of a true friend?

1. Play the *Go to the Wall* game. Identify one wall as the YES side and one wall as the NO side. Ask students to indicate their response to the following questions (given verbally, one at a time) by going to one wall or the other:

What would you do for a friend?

- Would you let your friend copy your homework?
- Would you let your friend borrow your compact discs for his or her vacation?
- Would you not tell on a friend you saw stealing from a store?
- Would you babysit for a friend so that she or he could go to a party?
- Would you run out to help a friend who fell off a bike on a busy street?

2. Study the Bible to discover more about the friendship of Jonathan and David. Invite the students to read the text from their Bibles. This can be done silently, or have a volunteer read for the group. Ask them to be watching for how the three characters–Jonathan, David, and Saul–felt in this story.

- What risks did Jonathan take?
- How do you think he decided to side with his friend?
- What might have happened had he not supported David?

When the reading is complete, assign partners or groups to work on preparing a newsclip interview with one of the characters. One partner will take the role of the reporter, and one, the role of the character. Encourage them to work together on the preparation of the questions and answers. Let them practice their interview once they feel they are ready. Then take turns presenting the interviews to the entire group. If you have access to a video recorder, it would be a great way to present the interviews. Allow them to watch themselves on the video and discuss what they learned about how "their" character felt.

3. Encourage thinking about friendship by having the students respond to the following questions:

- What do you learn about friendship from this situation?
- Do you think there are situations today that are similar where a friend needs to choose between a parent and a friend?
- Did Jonathan do the right thing by disobeying his father?

Distribute several construction-paper heart shapes to each student. Ask each person to write a quality that is important in a best friend on each heart shape. Encourage them to use as many shapes as they can. After a brief time of individual writing and thinking, ask them to come together and invite them to take turns posting each heart on a large bristol or poster board heart or a bulletin board entitled "A True Friend Is...." After each has shared or posted their hearts, ask them to think of someone their own age and someone not their own age who has shown some of these qualities to them. Looking at those qualities, decide together how God demonstrates those qualities as well.

Reflect and Remember

Following whatever ritual you have established, invite the students to spend a few minutes of quiet, individual time talking with God. Imagine God to be as close and understanding as a best friend.

Take a Break (15 min.)

1. Have a snack.
2. Play a favourite active game or just stretch and relax.

Respond (45 min.)

1. Continue whatever ongoing craft you have chosen.

2. Carry out the visit planned yesterday. A service project is a great way to become actively involved in loving God by loving others. Be affirming of all of the youth's efforts, whether great or small. Their willingness and participation is a way of expressing love as well.

3. Encourage your group to develop a game that illustrates one aspect of friendship. Alternatively, they could take a common active, competitive game and rewrite the rules so that it can be played more cooperatively. Encourage them to try not only their new game but also to identify how the process felt for them. Were there any problems with the game or the rules? What was better about the new way of playing?

Gather and Bless (15 min.)

Continue with your closing ritual. Review the posted memory verses.

Sample interview questions.

Session 3, Study and Discuss #2

JONATHAN

1. What risks did you encounter in your friendship with David?

2. How did you feel about needing to choose between your father and your best friend?

3. How do you think you might continue your friendship with David?

DAVID

1. How do you feel about what your friend Jonathan did for you?

2. Do you think you should continue to be friends with Jonathan, since you are both in a dangerous situation?

SAUL

1. How do you feel about David and Jonathan's friendship?

2. Why did you not like David?

Session 4

Abigail

Theme: Loving God by Making Peace
Bible Text: 1 Samuel 25:1-38
Story Focus: Abigail demonstrated creative thinking skills in order to keep peace between two enemies, Nabal and David.
Faith Focus: We show we love God when we solve our problems in peaceful ways.

Get Ready

1. Gather supplies for making a peace promise mural or peace T-shirts. See Respond, page 198.
2. Collect props for Study and Discuss #3. Some items to include in each box are the following: baseball or soccer equipment such as a ball and glove, young children's toys, snack food such as chocolate bars of obviously different sizes, popular items of clothing such as a brand-name hat or shirt.
3. Have a large chart and markers handy. Placards, sticks, and markers are needed for Study and Discuss #1.

Gather and Greet (15 min.)

Greet each person warmly. Distribute name tags. As preparation for the theme of the session, provide a large chart and markers. Invite the students to try to fill the chart with the names of famous peacemakers. Ask them to be watching the Bible story drama to find out how this particular peacemaker, Abigail, operated.

Worship

Go together as a group to Worship. Participate with enthusiasm.

Study and Discuss (45 min.)

We encounter conflict situations often. Help the students experience and learn peaceful and creative ways of solving problems. How do we show our love for God by working at and for peace?

1. Focus on how Abigail came up with creative solutions to a problem. Do this short exercise to help the participants think about and experience conflict resolution.

   a. Read or review the fairy tale of "The Three Little Pigs." A humourous version, *The True Story of the Three Little Pigs, by A. Wolf* as told to Jon Scieszka (Viking Children's Books, 1989) would be appropriate. This book presents the wolf's viewpoint.

   b. Ask for one or two volunteers to be observers. Divide the rest of the students into two groups. One group will represent the pigs, and the other will represent the wolf. Each group will need a large placard on a stick and markers.

   c. Ask each group to think of the "rights" that pertain to their character (e.g., pigs may have the right to build a house without harassment; a wolf may have the right to hunt in the forest). Give them about two minutes to list as many rights as possible on their placards and then begin marching about the room, calling out their slogans or "bill of rights."

   d. Ask the two observers to come up with ways to solve the conflict peacefully so that both the pigs and the wolf feel satisfied.

   e. Invite everyone to join the discussion and to suggest possible solutions.

   f. Evaluate the solutions as a group. Were we able to come up with a fair solution to this problem? Ask the observers to explain how they felt about their role. Ask the participants to evaluate their feelings about the observers' attempts to make peace. Point out that feelings of anger and hurt come about when anyone feels he or she is treated unfairly.

2. Study the Bible together to examine Abigail's methods of peacemaking. Listen for the answers to the following questions as the leader reads the text as expressively as possible. Encourage the youth to follow the story in their own Bibles.

- What was the reason for the conflict?
- What did Abigail do to resolve the conflict?
- What might have been some of the options she could have chosen?
- What could the men in this situation have done to prevent this conflict from occurring?

3. Encourage the youth to come up with creative ways of solving conflicts that they may have dealt with in their own lives.

   a. Have available enough "prop boxes" so that there is one box for each group of three to four students. See Get Ready #2.

   b. Each group uses the props in its assigned box to create a skit that somehow portrays a conflict situation. Allow the groups time to brainstorm and come up with their own situation. They should not show the resolution of the conflict.

   c. When the groups are ready, ask one group at a time to present its skit to the remainder of the class.

   d. At the end of each skit, ask the entire group to offer as many solutions as possible to this conflict. Affirm each group's participation and effort, and help the youth to discover which of the solutions offer an opportunity to both parties to feel good about the resolution of the conflict through win-win solutions.

Reflect and Remember

Form a circle. Talk briefly about the meaning of confession as a type of prayer. We need to ask God's forgiveness when we do not solve problems in the best way.

Mention that you will be making four statements or thoughts. There will be a short time of silence after each one when the youth will have opportunity to reflect and pray silently.

Create a sense of quiet reverence. Quiet music could be played, or sing "Lord, Listen to Your Children Praying" as an introduction to the prayer time. Invite the students to participate in a time of prayer together.

Present the following thoughts:

1. Think of a time when you did something that hurt someone. Tell God you are sorry for what you did. Plan how you will tell the person you are sorry. Ask God to help you follow through on your plan to ask forgiveness of someone.

2. Think of a time when you did not stop a fight or argument between others. Tell God you are sorry for not being a peacemaker. In your imagination, step in and be a peacemaker in that situation. Decide how you can be a better peacemaker when you are faced with a similar situation. Ask God to help you stay true to your promise.

3. Think of a time when you did not want to do the right thing. Ask God to help you make decisions that bring peace to you, your family, and to others. Decide how you will know what is the right thing to do. Ask for God's wisdom and strength to help you.

4. Think of a time when you did the right thing to solve a problem. Thank God for helping you to be a creative thinker and problem solver. Promise God that you will continue to be a peacemaker.

Close with a verbal prayer from the leader, thanking God for the assurance of forgiveness and God's promise to help us solve our problems in God's way of peace.

Take a Break (15 min.)

1. Have a snack.
2. Enjoy a time of active games or just relaxing.

Respond (45 min.)

1. Continue with your chosen ongoing craft.
2. Choose one of the following activities:

Make a Peace Promise Mural

Give the youth the opportunity to symbolize their commitment to peace in a visible way by placing peace promises and their footprints on a giant mural. Use a large piece of newsprint or cloth (bedsheet or old tablecloth). Allow the students to write peace-slogan symbols or the Scripture verse on the mural. Pour or mix poster paints in flat baking pans large enough for a foot. Also have warm, soapy water and some towels available.

Invite each person to make one footprint by dipping her or his foot into the paint and placing it on the mural. Provide water and towels for the students to wash and dry their feet. If desired, the students can print their names with markers beside their footprints. Allow the mural to dry, then post or hang it for all to see.

Make a Peace T-Shirt

Provide either fabric crayons, fabric markers, or bubble paint suitable for use on fabric. Encourage the students to decorate the shirt with peace symbols, such as the dove (below), or peacemaking quotes or rules. Be open to lots of creativity!

Gather and Bless (15 min.)

Continue with your usual ritual and closing blessing.

Permission is granted to purchasers of this curriculum to photocopy this page for use with the Loving God *curriculum.*

Session 5

David

Theme: Loving God by Showing Kindness
Bible Text: 2 Samuel 4:4; 9:1-13
Story Focus: David showed kindness and brought Mephibosheth into his home.
Faith Focus: We show we love God when we are kind, just, and generous.

Get Ready

1. Bring a snack of single-serving items for Study and Discuss.
2. Copy the Kindness Quiz Cards, page 204. Make enough copies so that every child may have one card.
3. Gather items for playing *The Feast of David* game, page 202.
4. Check Respond #4 and set up equipment for showing one of the videos.
5. Write the ratings for Study and Discuss #4 on chart paper or the board.

Gather and Greet (15 min.)

Distribute name tags if still needed. As preparation for the last story and theme, do a brief review of all the stories and themes. Ask the group to share a time when someone was very kind to them even though they may have felt they did not deserve this kindness.

Study and Discuss (45 min.)

Loving God requires us to do justice and to love kindness as the theme and memory text state. Opportunities will be given to both experience and discuss the ideas of kindness and generosity.

1. Sharing snacks. Have available a bowl of a variety of single-serving-size goodies; e.g., chocolate bar, apple, can of pop, package of crackers. Make sure that there is one less snack or treat than there are students. Keep one large bag of chips or popcorn in reserve, out of sight. Put up a sign near the bowl: "Help

Yourself!" As the students begin to help themselves to the snack, appear to ignore what they are doing and go on with other tasks. As a problem becomes apparent, begin a discussion with the group:

- How do you feel about the snack you got?
- How do you feel about the snack others got?
- Did sharing happen?
- How were justice, kindness, and generosity shown?

If one person did not get a snack, you may offer the large bag of chips to the person who did not get a fair share of the original goodies. Allow some time to observe the group's reactions. Will kindness, justice, and generosity now be displayed by the person who has received something that could be shared? Again, use some of the same questions to discuss feelings. Help the group avoid personal put-downs. Encourage each student to focus on her or his own actions and feelings. Be sure to make clear the purpose of this exercise: to understand how we react in situations where kindness, justice, and generosity need to be acted upon.

2. Read the text directly from the Bible. Either have the students read it silently or have a volunteer read it aloud for the group. Think about how kindness, justice, and generosity were shown in today's story of David and Mephibosheth. Note that in the days of David, a crippled person would normally be seen as a social outcast. Clarify David's response to Mephibosheth as one of unusual kindness, not duty.

Ask everyone to be ready to respond to the following questions:

- What is one thing that surprised you about this story?
- What are your questions about this story?

3. Discuss the Bible text. Talk about the kind of justice David showed. David looked after his friend's son because it was the right thing to do. He showed kindness to Mephibosheth because it was the right thing to do. God expects us to "love kindness" and do acts of kindness because it is the right thing to do. Kindness is a way to show that we love God. Acts of loving-kindness are not always easy. We may not always feel kind. To act kindly may not always be the "fair" way, but it is the right way. To show kindness means to show respect for one another, to treat the other person the way you wish to be treated, to consider each person to be of equal value.

4. Copy the Kindness Quiz Cards, page 204. Invite the students to draw one quiz card and then write at least four to five possible responses. The question to be answered is: "What would be an act of loving-kindness that I could do if I were in this situation?"

After each response, give it a code as follows:

E—easy to do, but not too helpful
GH—good idea, but hard to do
N—no way do I think I could ever do that
JR—just right idea

After the students have had a chance to respond individually on their quiz cards, invite them to come together again as a group. Ask each individual to tell all of his or her responses without revealing their ratings.

Read each situation and allow the rest of the group to vote on what rating they think is appropriate. Tally all the votes on the chalkboard for each situation.

Talk about the difference between doing an act of kindness out of generosity or only doing what is fair.

Take a Break (15 min.)

1. Have a snack.
2. Choose your group's favourite way of relaxing.

Respond (45 min.)

1. Continue with the ongoing craft. Offer ample time that the project can be completed and that the students are able to take home their completed item. If you are making the banner or quilt that will be hung in the facilities, find a suitable place to display the items you have made. Allow the students to feel the satisfaction of having completed a fine gift.

2. Plan to carry out your service project. There would be many people, churches, or agencies who would appreciate an act of loving-kindness from the junior youth. There may be clothes to sort at your local thrift store or opportunities to serve at a nearby soup kitchen. Perhaps something as simple as helping to clean up on the last day of your *Loving God* programme would provide an opportunity to put loving-kindness into action.

3. Choose one of the following games to play with your group:

The Feast of David

a. Number the children to form groups of five. Assign numbers to each of the five persons in the group, beginning with the tallest: #1 will be Mephibosheth, #2 David, #3 Abigail, #4 Zodiac, #5 Ziba.
b. Ahead of time, set up the "stage" for the game. Mark off an area with ropes to represent the ditch. Abigail (Person #3) is on the one side (palace side) holding a treat for the others on her team. Across the ditch is a narrow piece of wood. Set the planks at a distance of about 3 meters, 3 yards, from each other so there is room for each group to move. (See illustration, page 80, Talk and Move.)
c. Give this introduction: David and Abigail live in the king's palace. Around the palace is a ditch filled with quicksand. The bridge that people normally use to get into the palace was wrecked in a freak windstorm. A narrow plank of wood is the only way to get across this ditch. One's life is in danger if one steps off the plank. Abigail is on the palace side ready to host a great feast in honour of Mephibosheth's arrival. David and Mephibosheth, along with the two servants, are on the other side of the ditch and are very anxious to get to the feast.
d. Follow these rules for the game:
   - All people must play the role of the character they were assigned.
   - If someone steps off the plank, the group must all return to the other side, except for Abigail.
   - Being a polite hostess, Abigail will not serve the feast until her entire group is assembled on the palace side of the ditch.
   - Mephibosheth has his legs tied together at the ankle so he cannot walk by himself.
e. Play the game.

f. Debrief. Sit together for discussion. Ask people to tell how they felt playing the role of the character to which they were assigned? How did Mephibosheth feel? How did you feel about Mephibosheth? What were the creative ways used to get across the ditch? Did anyone think about putting the planks together and working together with another group?

Disability Soccer or Volleyball

Play a common, popular game such as soccer or volleyball. The variation will be that each person will play with a "visible disability" at some point during the game. Distribute disabilities randomly during the game, such as the following: blindfold someone, someone sits on a chair, someone wears earmuffs, someone wears large boots or a helmet.

Debrief. How did you like the game? What did you learn about yourself and your feelings of competition? How did you act towards people who had a disability? How were you able to treat everyone equally and with the same respect? What did you learn about loving-kindness through this game?

Reflect and Remember

Allow some time at the end of the session for a wrap-up time. Before your closing ritual, express your appreciation and love to the junior youth. Affirm them and encourage them to continue listening to and talking with God. As we do so, our friendship with God grows stronger and we become better people. Review together the prayers and/or memory texts of the week. Encourage each person to find a quiet place and reflect on God's friendship in their own way. Play quiet music and allow several minutes for this time of reflection. Then invite the group to join together and respond to these questions:

- Which activity did you like best during our *Loving God* programme? Why?
- Which of the characters did you identify with the most? Why?
- What did you learn about loving God?

Gather and Bless (15 min.)

End with your closing blessing and a group hug.

Take time to copy, fill out, and mail the evaluation form on page 205.

Kindness Quiz Cards

You are picking teams for soccer with your friends. Chris, who is much shorter than the rest of the kids in the class, comes along and asks to play with everyone. The captain of one of the teams replies, "Naw, we need someone who can run pretty fast on our side. Better wait until you grow up a bit!"

Response ________________ Rating ____

Nathan, one of the boys in your class, has been missing a lot of school lately. When he returns to school, the teacher takes some time to talk to the class and informs the kids that Nathan has been diagnosed with cancer, and will likely need to have extra support from kids to keep his work caught up.

Response ________________ Rating ____

When you get home from school, your mom is lying on the couch feeling sick. There is no snack or supper ready, and your younger sister's diaper and clothes are a mess.

Response ________________ Rating ____

After a bad snowstorm, you notice one of your elderly neighbours out clearing the snow from her car. She is having a hard time chipping away the ice.

Response ________________ Rating ____

Your best friend has just told you that her parents are going to separate and likely will get a divorce.

Response ________________ Rating ____

You meet a person who is homeless. You find out that this person sleeps at the bus station.

Response ________________ Rating ____

Permission is granted to purchasers of this curriculum to photocopy this page for use with the Loving God *curriculum.*

Curriculum Evaluation Form

Loving God

Church ____________________

Address ____________________

Evaluator ____________________

Leadership role ____________________

Use of materials: Age-group

_____five-day Bible school ____________

_____Sunday school ____________

_____midweek classes ____________

_____festival or retreat ____________

other __________________ ____________

Describe your experience with these materials—the process, the positive aspects, the problems. (Use the back side for additional comments.)

List any suggestions to improve these materials.

Thank-you. Your input is greatly appreciated.

Please return completed form to Living Stones Collection, Commission on Education, General Conference Mennonite Church, Box 347, Newton, KS 67114.

(*Loving God,* Copyright © 1996, Faith and Life Press, Newton, KS 67114. All rights reserved. Printed in the U.S.A. Permission is granted to photocopy this page.)